GROWN WOMAN 101

GUIDE FOR BECOMING
AN EXTRAORDINARY WOMAN

MARITA KINNEY

GROWN WOMAN

101

How to be an Extraordinary Woman

By Marita Kinney

Pure Thoughts Publishing, LLC

Copyright

The information provided herein is stated to be truthful and consistent, in that any liability, in terms of inattention or otherwise, by any usage or abuse of any policies, processes, or directions contained within is the solitary and utter responsibility of the recipient reader. Under no circumstances will any legal responsibility or blame be held against the publisher for any reparation, damages, or monetary loss due to the information herein, either directly or indirectly.

Respective authors own all copyrights not held by the publisher.

The information herein is offered for informational purposes solely, and is universal as so. The presentation of the information is without contract or any type of guarantee assurance.

Library of Congress Control Number: 2016934070

All Rights Reserved. ISBN-13: 978-1943409105

Table of Contents

Grown Woman 101

Grown Woman 101

Grown Woman 101

Grown Woman 101

Dedication

I dedicate this book to my beautiful daughters:

Jerney Lynn, You remind me so much of myself. You have a sweet spirit and quiet confidence. Baby girl, you don't have to do anything to get anyone's attention, the world sees you. Not just your beauty, but your heat. I absolutely love you, lady bug. Whenever I feel like quitting, I look at you and remember that I can't… because you're watching me. Thank you for loving me and always offering to take an extra load off of me. My sidekick, assistant, and oldest daughter; keep cooking, styling hair, and doing anything that makes you smile, they are all worth pursuing.

Anisa Lynn, I have tears in my eyes as I write this. You have been the star in my life on some of my darkest days. God has given you a gift for cheering people up. You truly are a super star. I have never met a person as confident as you. I have always admired your boldness. You are full of life and I'm blessed to have you as my daughter. People remember you because of how you make them feel. Continue to put smiles upon the people's faces, but don't ever forget to keep one for yourself. I love you, Sweet Pea.

Shiloh Marie, My independent sweet baby girl. I'll never forget when you were 8 months and began walking on Mother's Day. You are strong willed and determined to do whatever is in your heart. You have ambition and determination, just like your father. Your smile is priceless and you give the best hugs. You are extremely intelligent and always wanting to learn new things. Promise to teach others along the way. You will one day discover that life will be your greatest teacher. Pay attention and look to God for all of the answers. Spread your wings, my sweet butterfly, life is waiting on you. I love you, always and forever.

Shay Alexandria, To my Baby Bumble Bee, my youngest of six children, my amazing daughter. Shay, you too, are a lot like me. You even have freckles on your hands, just like me. You are shy, yet very outgoing, sensitive, but also strong. You are the perfect mixture of me and your father. You sing when no one is watching and dance in private. Watching you discover your gifts has been one of my greatest joys. You are my quiet storm. Have you ever wondered why I call you my Baby Bumble Bee? Because you are small, but also have a sting if someone crosses you the wrong way. Continue to sing praises to God. Even when you think no one hears you, He does. I love you.

I have always taught you girls to love God, always be ladylike, stand up for yourself, pray for those who hurt you, and to always stay true to who you truly are.

Love, Mom

Introduction

Being a grown woman has absolutely nothing to do with your chronological age. The ability of understanding that is the first and most critical step in your process. Yes! Every one of us has a process that we must go through in order to reach the status of an extraordinary grown woman. As you evolve into who you are supposed to become, you will learn to appreciate your personal journey into womanhood. Growing and evolving as a woman doesn't always feel good. Lessons can be extremely harsh and brutal. I promise that nothing you have been through is in vain. If applied correctly, the lessons will be used to mold you into the woman that you are destined to become. Your journey is connected to our purpose. Embrace your scars, love your war marks, and even fall in love with your stretch marks.

I didn't write this book because I'm an expert on this subject. However, I am a woman who has begun to understand my own journey through womanhood as I travel and speak across the country, meet awesome women, and relate to their pain. It hasn't taken long for me to discover that all these women are extraordinary. The only problem is that they can't see it. This book is written to magnify your greatness, not your flaws. We all have a countless number of flaws, but overlook the essence of our greatness. Today, I pray that you embrace the things that make you different. It all starts with your perspective of you.

RESPONSIBILITY

Chapter One: Taking Responsibility

Becoming a grown woman is not determined by your chronological age. It is a state of being, not existing, a state of becoming and constantly evolving into a woman. When you review your life, I'm pretty sure that you will be able to point out a lot of errors. You can probably recall a lot of mistakes and also regrets. Along with that, I'm sure you have shifted the blame onto others. I'm guilty of doing that too. No one wants to own up to their poor judgment, or be forced to look at immature female habits. You know the habits I'm referring to. I'm talking about bad relationship habits, bad spending habits, bad eating habits, bad parenting habits, bad spiritual habits, and any other habit that have consistently caused you terrible failure. Whatever you do effortlessly, over and over again, becomes your routine or habit. We all have good habits, but pretend that we don't realize our bad ones.

Why do we shift the blame to other people? The answer is simple. We do this because it helps us to feel better. It's a defense mechanism that allows us to avoid looking at ourselves. If you have to look at yourself, you're then forced to face the truth. What is that truth? That's completely up to you to decide. You have perceptions of your life. Oftentimes, your perceptions stop you from taking the blame for the things that you don't like in your life, when in reality, you have shaped your own life more than you actually realize. Think about all the decisions that you have made. Think about all of the people that you have allowed to influence you. Yes, I said 'allowed to influence you'. You see, a lot of times we are at fault for what influences us. The things we watch, the people we listen to, the people we choose to be friends with, the jobs we choose, the mentors we choose, the places where we choose to live. There are so many things that we have allowed to influence where we currently are in life.

How many times have you looked at the TV and had a bright idea? It could be something as simple as watching a home television show and getting creative ideas for decorating your home. You allowed that show to influence you, one way or another. I'm not saying that influences are bad. I'm just saying that you should take responsibility for the influences that are coming into your life. Now, this book is not going to be one of those books that is going to make you feel all warm and bubbly on the inside. No, this book is going to help you to examine yourself so that you can become the extraordinary woman that you desire to be. You know the woman I'm referring to. The woman that is deep inside, at your core. The woman that you're so afraid of, and the woman who isn't afraid of her purpose and will achieve it, no matter the necessary price. It's like she's sitting deep down inside of you, and you can't find her. You can't release her, but you know she's there, because sometimes she allows you to explore a little bit. Then right when you are about to find her, she hides. The question is, have you given her the freedom to be free? You have a spirit inside of your body, and your spirit is the purest form of you that is directly connected to God.

Oftentimes, we are made up of so many layers that we cannot strip them all away to get to the true essence of the extraordinary woman that we are. We are so bogged down with life's responsibilities, like relationships, children, and work, and we tend to forget who we truly are outside of those daily duties. Maybe it's not forgetting who you are. Maybe it's not identifying who you are. Nevertheless, I'm going to help you.

Taking responsibility for your life means that you have to take 100% responsibility for everything. What does that mean? Now, this is really scary. Can you imagine taking 100% responsibility for every area of your life? You have to, in order to mature. You have to realize where you went wrong and where you went right. Now, I know some people may evaluate their lives and say, 'Well, Marita, it's really hard to take responsibility for certain instances in my childhood, because I was violated." You may have been molested, or had other terrible things like that happen to you.

Please allow me to clarify. Taking responsibility is not excusing the offender, but it's saying, "I've allowed myself to be a victim all these years, instead of recognizing that I'm actually a survivor." A child is innocent, but you can take responsibility for allowing that pain to hurt you daily. Oftentimes, women will get well into their thirties, but have allowed the pain to control their lives. You have to take responsibility for allowing the pain to continuously control your life.

Now, I know this seems harsh, but when someone hurts you, yes, they have done what they have done, and some of these things are awful, but when you continue to pour salt in your own wounds by not allowing yourself to heal, you are guilty every single day for hurting yourself. Now, listen, I'm not insensitive, but I have to share with you that it's important to realize that you have a choice. A lot of people who have been victimized re-live it daily and let it become their identity. They dismiss the choice they have to no longer be held captive by the ghosts from their past. I'm here to tell you that you do have choice. Whatever is holding you back from becoming the best version of yourself has to be defeated, or it will defeat you.

That one incident should not become your identity, but if you have allowed it to, that's no one's fault but your own. You cannot let a moment define your whole entire life. It's not who you are. Things happen to us, but we are not defined by a moment in time. It's very hard to take responsibility for the things that hurt us. I will say again, what you're taking responsibility for is the reaction; not the cause, but the effect.

As you read this book, you're going to realize that you have more power than you give yourself credit for. You have more strength than you acknowledge. You have more wisdom that you share. Life experiences will teach you something that no college degree will ever teach. I challenge you, as you read through this book, to look at the various concepts that are shared, and examine your life and take responsibility, so that you can have the life that you truly desire to have, and step in to the extraordinary woman that you know you are.

Reflection: What are three areas in your life that you can take responsibility for?

Example: I was a teenage mother and I use to blame my parents for not properly educating me about sex and not showing an interest in my life at that time, which made me feel overlooked, and like they failed to help me understand my value. Once I DECIDED to take responsibility for my life, I chose to no longer blame my parents for my early sexual behavior. Although the things that I shared about my parents were true, it wasn't fair that I shifted all of the blame onto them. I knew that having sex could lead to having a baby. I wasn't naïve; I only pretended to be in order to not take any responsibility for my teenage pregnancy. It wasn't my parents that I had to forgive. I had to learn how to forgive myself for the decisions that I once made.

And ye shall know the truth, and the truth shall make you free. John 8:32

Chapter Two: Taking Responsibility for Your Life

I know we just talked about taking responsibility overall, but let's get really specific. There are things in your life - now I don't know what these things are, but you do - that are critical for you to own up to, because you cannot *grow* past it until you *grow* through it. Not *go* through it. You've already gone through it. Now, I'm asking you to give yourself permission to grow through it.

What are you going through? Think about the things in your life and in your past that have hindered you emotionally, physically, spiritually, or just have kept you stuck in a place of sadness or depression. I want you to think of these things. For me, it was my teen pregnancy. For a long time, I blamed my parents for not spending enough time with me. At one point, I blamed my mother for not educating me enough about relationships and boys. I blamed my father for being a preacher and not allowing me to date. When I was younger, I was just very happy to have a boyfriend, and now I had to do all the things that the other girlfriends were doing. I blamed everybody for my situation. Actually, it wasn't until I was almost 28 or 29 years old that I realized that I had all of this discreet blame towards my parents that they were unaware of. They had no idea that I blamed them for my becoming a teenage parent.

Although having my son was a life changing moment for me, which forever impacted my life in a positive way, it also reminded me of how sad I was throughout my teenage years, of being pregnant and being judged, and all of those things. As a teenager, I really wasn't prepared to be judged in the way that I was. I was angry, and it wasn't until I started to do some self-evaluations and take responsibility for my life that I came to the conclusion that I had falsely accused my parents.

In reality, I knew how babies were made. I knew that if I had sex, there was a possibility that I could get pregnant. I knew this, but it felt better to force the blame on someone else. We all have done it. It felt so good to not take responsibility for getting pregnant. It was so much easier for me to say, "Yeah, my parents did this, or my parents didn't do that." That was so much easier, but to face the fact that I become pregnant at an early age because of my actions was a hard pill to swallow, because that part of my life shaped so many things that happened afterward.

This book is really not about my life, but I wanted to share that example with you on how I forced the blame on other people for a long time. What are you doing with your life? Are you blaming someone for where you live? Are you blaming someone because of the education you received? Are you blaming someone for not loving you? Are you blaming an ex-husband for leaving you? Who are you blaming and for what?

This is an exercise that I actually started to do with my daughters. Now, I'm a mother of six children, as well as raising my niece. I have two sons and four daughters, and because of my experiences, I can help my daughters take responsibility for very important things, because I want them to be those extraordinary women that I try to help other women be. I want my daughters to become that. They tattletale on each other all day, let me tell you. Oh my goodness, they can argue for days, but they'll run to me and they'll tell me what the other sister did. I'll stop them in their tracks and say, "Wait a minute. Wait a minute. Hold on. Before you begin to tell me what your sister did, I want to tell you, I'm not interested. I'm only interested in what you did. Tell me, what did you do?"

Of course, they never want to tell me what they did, but I will not accept anything other than what they have done. They have to sit there and tell me what they're responsible for, and then I'll look at the other sister and I'll go, "Okay, it's your turn. Tell me, what did you do?" Believe it or not, that exercise helps my daughters to look at themselves and how the situation could be different based on what they have done, not what the other person is doing.

That's something that's important, because it teaches individuals how to take responsibility. I want you to look over the different areas of your life. What are you responsible for? Oftentimes, we complain that we don't like the neighborhood we live in. Oftentimes, you chose to live there. I know somebody will say, "Well, Marita, I don't have the money to live anywhere else." You chose the job that gives you the income to live wherever it is you want to live.

You applied for that job. You knew how much they paid. The problem is that you don't think you can have more, but you haven't owned up to that either. You have to take responsibility and say, "I have the job that I have because I don't think that I qualify for anything else." If that's what you feel, you have to own up to it and say that that's how you feel.

When you take responsibility, it gives you an opportunity to change things. You can change your thought process. You can change jobs, and you can also move if you don't like where you're living. The problem is that people force the blame on someone else over and over again. Take responsibility for where you are right now in life.

Grown Woman 101

Who's Showing Up in Your Life TODAY?

Many of us women have many layers that have shaped who we are today. Those layers typically consist of life experiences, disappointments, accomplishments, and of course, some extremely deep wounds. Wounds have a tendency to stand out amongst your other layers. Why is it that we only see the pain, heartbreak, and agony in our lives? We seldom focus on the joyous occasions and happy moments. It's because whatever you focus on will be magnified.

Most of my hurt occurred in my early childhood. Due to this, I grew up looking for that familiar feeling in my adulthood. I waited for it. I expected it. I didn't know what life would feel like without it. I had no idea that I was living my life bonded to the little girl that still hurt inside of me. The hurt little girl was controlling my thoughts and essentially forming my adult perspective on life. She was shaping my world. The adult woman was held captive to the past. I was present in my life, the little girl inside me was. Everything was affected by this crazy illusion. The way I reacted to situations, my relationships, my dreams, my parenting, every aspect of my life was in bondage - until one day I decided to do something about it. I hated being insecure. I was ready to confront my internal conflict. The little girl inside of me was no longer welcomed into my sacred space.

The first step was to recognize who was *showing up* in my daily life. I had to be aware of every conversation and feeling. When I engaged in conversations with my husband and became offended, I had to learn how to differentiate who was responding. Was it the hurt eight-year-old little girl who felt abandoned by her mother, got picked on at school, and had low self-esteem, or was the person responding in the conversation the mature, confident, educated, classy, sophisticated, and emotional 33-year-old woman showing up?

Once I was conscious of the conflict, I was empowered to respond differently to situations. Before I spoke abruptly towards individuals, I thought about how I wanted to reply. I began to choose my words wisely, and calm the anxiety that came with my wounds. I began to mature, and eventually the little girl that used to throw temper tantrums inside of me was all out of excuses and finally grew up. I took control over my life and forfeited all of my defenses. I desperately wanted to be whole. Through Christ Jesus, I was able to able to forgive anyone who had hurt me. A shift and new perspective of my life had formulated in my spirit. For the first time in my life, I truly felt free.

Grown Woman 101

Sometimes we get into our way. We stop our own progress. Pain hurts, but if acknowledged correctly, it will turn into growing pain.   Every next level of your life demands and requires a different you. Who will show up? Everything you want is on the other side of fear. Don't be afraid to meet who you are becoming.

Don't Go Through Life, Grow Through It

In what ways are you still like a child?

What makes you react immaturely?

Can you allow your *adult-self* to speak in a manner that represents who you are today?

Can you let the little girl inside of you embrace your future instead of reliving the past?

1 Corinthians 13:11

When I was a child, I spoke and thought and reasoned as a child. But when I grew up, I put away childish things.

Chapter Three: Taking Responsibility for Your Finances

I cannot tell you how many times I've heard people complain about their credit and not having enough money, talking about how overwhelmed they are with their bills. When you begin to take responsibility for your finances, you're taking responsibility for your habits: your spending habits, your saving habits, your thinking habits, your income habits.

All of these are habits, and when you do them over and over again, that's what makes them habits. If you don't like them, you have an opportunity to change them, but you have to take responsibility and you have to realize that you have a decision. A lot of people blame their financial situation on their parents or someone from their childhood and say, "Well, my mother didn't tell teach me how to manage money, or we were always getting evicted, or I became a nurse because everyone in my family has become a nurse, but I have all this debt from school and I hate being a nurse."

The thing is, you have to realize that none of those things are anyone else's fault. You chose your career, because you wanted to choose it. If you chose it because of someone else in your family did it, you have to own up to that, and you have to realize why you're in the field that you are in that you hate so much. A lot of times, people end up in a career that's very popular in their family, instead of looking within themselves and trying to figure out what was it that they were really supposed to do. What was your purpose?

It's not too late to find out. However, if you're complaining about your job and the money you make, do something about it. Take responsibility. In our last chapter, you learned that you had a choice. You went to that job interview. You filled out that application. All those things that landed you that job, you did, so you have to take responsibility, even for the career that you supposedly hate and doesn't pay you enough right now.

Another thing that we struggle with is our credit and managing money. As much as we all love to blame our parents for this, there are so many classes and online references that we can utilize to educate ourselves on finances. If you fail to do that, then you have to take responsibility for that too. Say, "No, I would rather just use the excuse that I do things the way that I do because that's what I was taught or that's what I wasn't taught." If you want a different financial outcome, you have to do something differently.

What are you going to do differently? How is your day-to day-budget going to change? Do you want to have a savings goal? You may have to start packing your lunch instead of going out to eat with co-workers every day. You have to decide where you want to be, and then you have to be realistic about where you are. You have to come up with a plan to fill in the gap. Don't go broke trying to look rich.

This cannot happen until you truly take responsibility of where you currently are financially. What does your financial thermostat look like? Are you feeling well, or are you really, really sick? It takes time to build up bad credit and it's going to take time to fix it, so you can't just want things to happen overnight. It's going to take time to re-condition your thinking. A lot of people make the mistake in thinking that if they just have a lump sum of money, it's going to solve all of their problems.

That's the biggest misconception anyone who has financial issues can believe. It's not a money issue, it's a mindset issue. It's a money management issue. You can't borrow money. You can't beg for money, because if your mindset has not changed, you're going to end up in the exact same situation over and over again until you develop better habits. With that being said, I want you to review your financial situation and if it's good, what can you do to make it better?

If it's awful, what can you do to get yourself out of that awful state? Whatever it is you need to do, sit down with yourself, be realistic, and realize how you got into the situation that you are in. If you have a savings goal, think about what you need to do in order to meet it. Do you overspend? Do you buy miscellaneous stuff that means absolutely nothing, but yet want to have a savings?

Be honest with yourself. Do you really want X amount of dollars in savings? Is that what you really want? Because if you really want it, you can't give yourself mixed messages. You can't go out and buy everything you want if you have to put money towards your goal. I always say this: "money with a purpose." If your money has no purpose, you will spend it on miscellaneous items, and your goals more than likely will not be met.

Whatever your financial goals are, you have to give your money a purpose. Just like when you get paid and you have to set aside certain amount of money for your mortgage or your rent or your car note, whatever it is that you are obligated to pay, you have to set money aside to do that. Why? Because that money has a purpose. If you have a savings goal, set aside money with a purpose for that. If you want to get out of debt, start with the lowest debt that you have and pay that off, and then move to the next one and the next one.

That's called the snowball effect, and make sure that you've given your money a purpose so that you can pay that debt off realistically. While you're paying down your bills, stop spending. Take responsibility for your finances. No one can improve your life and what you want from it other than yourself. I encourage you today to review your finances, take responsibility for where you are, and make a plan for were you want to go.

Tips:

52 Week Money Challenge Saving Plan

week	Amount Deposited	Account Balance	Week	Amount Deposited	Account Balance
1	$1.00	$1.00	27	$27.00	$378.00
2	$2.00	$3.00	28	$28.00	$406.00
3	$3.00	$6.00	29	$29.00	$435.00
4	$4.00	$10.00	30	$30.00	$465.00
5	$5.00	$15.00	31	$31.00	$496.00
6	$6.00	$21.00	32	$32.00	$528.00
7	$7.00	$28.00	33	$33.00	$561.00
8	$8.00	$36.00	34	$34.00	$595.00
9	$9.00	$45.00	35	$35.00	$630.00
10	$10.00	$55.00	36	$36.00	$666.00
11	$11.00	$66.00	37	$37.00	$703.00
12	$12.00	$78.00	38	$38.00	$741.00
13	$13.00	$91.00	39	$39.00	$780.00
14	$14.00	$105.00	40	$40.00	$820.00
15	$15.00	$120.00	41	$41.00	$861.00
16	$16.00	$136.00	42	$42.00	$903.00
17	$17.00	$153.00	43	$43.00	$946.00
18	$18.00	$171.00	44	$44.00	$990.00
19	$19.00	$190.00	45	$45.00	$1,035.00
20	$20.00	$210.00	46	$46.00	$1,081.00
21	$21.00	$231.00	47	$47.00	$1,128.00
22	$22.00	$253.00	48	$48.00	$1,176.00
23	$23.00	$276.00	49	$49.00	$1,225.00
24	$24.00	$300.00	50	$50.00	$1,275.00
25	$25.00	$325.00	51	$51.00	$1,326.00
26	$26.00	$351.00	52	$52.00	$1,378.00

www.buildingourstory.com

- Add your savings amount into your bill budget. When you pay your savings account as if it's a bill, you'll be more motivated to save.

- Give your money a purpose, set some goals, and plan ahead.

- Money without a purpose will be misused.

Chapter Four: Taking Responsibility for Your Health

You have reached an important part of this book. The quality of life that you have is contingent on how well you treat your body. You only get one body! Repeat after me...

"I only get one body!"

Once you understand that, you'll begin to show your body gratitude. Each part of your body will be appreciated. Oftentimes, we aren't thankful for something until it's gone. Don't take your health for granted. How many times have you decided to make healthy changes, but didn't follow through? Don't be embarrassed, we are all guilty of this. The good news is that none of that matters anymore. A grown woman realizes that yesterday was yesterday and today is today. Today, make the choice to commit. Commit to your goals, commit to your healthy lifestyle. You don't have to wait until New Year's or Monday morning to get started. You can get started right now. Whatever your health goals are, write them down. After you do that, sign and date it. Weight or unhealthiness is not your problem. Understand the root issue. YOU. Only you can make these changes. You lack commitment.

Sometimes we as women are afraid to change our appearance. I know and I get it. However, that's also part of maturing and embracing different seasons in your life. Honey, the reality is that your appearance will change at some point in time. Grow up and own it. There is not a cream or potion on this earth that will stop that.

A lot of times we want a certain quality of life, but realistically, we can't have the life that we truly desire if we don't feel good. One instance, my husband bought me a Jaguar for my birthday. Oh my goodness, I was so happy, and this Jaguar was beautiful. I couldn't believe he had bought this car for me, but he did, it was my birthday, and I was very grateful.

The only bad thing was that I didn't know that I was going to be as sick as was when I went to the dealership. I had some type of 24-hour bug, and here I was at the car dealership, picking up my brand new, all-white Jaguar and I was throwing up in the parking lot. It was awful. I remember the car salesman saying, "Is your wife pregnant?"

My husband and I looked at each other and said, "No," because we already had six kids and we knew that getting pregnant was not an option - unless God just miraculously wanted to do that, which I didn't think He would do to us - but nevertheless, here I was at this car dealership, throwing up in the parking lot because I had the flu, and not to mention, I had to drive this new car all the way home, which was about 40 minutes away. The new car scent that everybody loves, yeah, it didn't sit well with me having the flu, definitely not.

I was very sick and had to drive my car home, but I didn't want to leave it on the lot either. We have that new car syndrome, where we think, 'I don't want to leave the car on the lot, because they might say something didn't work out and try to keep it.' I wanted to get it home. I remember rolling down the window to let the wind blow on my face as I was driving home, and I was just so sick and didn't feel good.

I wanted to pick my kids up from school in this brand new car, but I was so sick that I couldn't. I just wanted to go home and lay down. I was reminded of how important my health was, because we want certain things in life, we want to travel, we want to do things, and we have to have things. It doesn't matter if we're sick. If we can't physically enjoy the moment, then it's not as pleasurable.

I went home and laid down, and I was in bed for about a day or so. When I felt better, I had a whole new experience with my car. I wanted to share that story with you, because the things that you really want in life will not be as pleasurable if you're sick. I know people are facing different illnesses, and some things we have contributed to because of our eating habits and our failure to exercise. There are so many things that we have to take responsibility for.

It's important that we take our health seriously, because we only get one body. We don't get another one. Weight here in the United States is an issue. A lot of people want to fit into that dress, or they want to be a certain size or weight, but they are not willing to do what it takes to attain that ideal weight and size. You have to take responsibility for that. Did you contribute to where you are physically right now? The answer is yes.

If you don't like something about your body, change it. If you are living with a condition, find out all that you can to help yourself improve, whether it's eating differently, exercising, changing your sleep habits, or something else. Stop complaining about your health and do something about it. A lot of times, it's not just your physical health, but it's a spiritual problem. Sometimes it's an emotional or mental problem. A lot of people are depressed now. You have to take responsibility.

What's causing you to feel depressed? Is it your friendships? Is it your family? Is it your job? It is your relationship? Find out what it is that's bringing you down. You decide if you want to allow that to continue to be in your life or not. You have to take responsibility for every area of your health. The reason why a lot of people don't want to take responsibility is because they don't want to have to be the one to change it to make a difference.

If you don't change and make things different, who will? No one can exercise for you but you. I wish I could sit here and do 100 sit-ups for you, but I can't. I love vegetables and I love salads. I wish I could eat all those things for you, but I can't. You have to do those things for you. I wish that some of the things that I have to do, you could do for me, but you cannot.

I have to take responsibility and do those things for myself. My husband can't do them. My children can't do them. My mum can't do them. No one can do them for me, but me. The same is true for you. Decide what your health goals are, where you are, and where you want to be, and do something different to change them. The first thing you have to do is look at yourself face-to-face and ask, 'what have I done to contribute to where I am right now?'

Even if you are built like a bodybuilder, don't overlook those accomplishments. Take responsibility. You worked hard. You are in good health because you take care of yourself. You are in good health because you are very health-conscious with what you eat and the nourishments that you give your body. Take responsibility. Give yourself credit. Stop giving your trainer credit. You're doing the work. Your trainer can't do the work for you. They are pushing you, but at the end of the day, you have done the work to get the results that you have.

Listen, taking responsibility is not all bad. Sometimes we just have to take responsibility for the things that we've done right. Pat yourself on the back, even if you're not where you want to be right now. You're reading this book. You need to pat yourself on the back and say, "I'm doing this. I'm going to take responsibility for my life, and I'm going to claim it and will get it back on track, and I will meet my goals to become the extraordinary woman that I know I am." It starts today with your health so that you can enjoy everything else that is part of your life.

Chapter Five: Taking Responsibility for Your Home

Decluttering Your Home

Have you ever noticed that you cannot find anything in your home; stuff is everywhere and you have an abundance of everything? Some people may call you a pack rat, or just simply tell you that you need a better system of organization. Well, from time to time we need to clean our house and declutter it to stay sane. The reality is that our homes are a reflection of how we really feel, deep down inside. As a result, we outwardly display our feelings and emotions in our habitat.

I will be the first to admit that I used to struggle with this and I wasn't sure why. I tried to organize things, but it always seemed as though I would run out of room, or couldn't find my items a particular spot in the house. This then made me realize that I had way too much stuff and needed to do something about it. So, my initial thought was to get rid of all of my unnecessary belongings that served absolutely no purpose in my home. However, I knew that this was not going to eliminate the issue, but only provide a temporary solution until I found myself right in the same boat again. Therefore, I chose to pray about it. Yeah, I know... Not trying to be all deep, but I had a feeling that the problem was something bigger going on inside of me that I was not aware of. After taking the situation to God, I then realized what the problem was, and felt the need to share this epiphany with you.

God revealed to me that people have an abundance of unnecessary things because they *don't trust him to supply it again.* Wow, this blew my mind. Essentially what happens is that we hold onto things too long due to the fear of that they will never be replaced. We don't realize that since God has blessed you with these things, shouldn't we trust him to do it again? We hold onto things for years with the hope of "maybe" using them again, when in the meantime, another family could have been blessed with them and has a need for them today. The problem is that we don't trust that we will get it back, so we hesitate to release it. "But this I say, He which soweth sparingly shall reap also sparingly; and he which soweth bountifully shall reap also bountifully." 2 Corinthians 9:6

I was shown that in order for God to continue to bless me and my family, I had to learn how to give more. It's a blessing to be a blessing to others. The truth of the matter is that the more that we give, the more that God will bless us with. It's a simple rule; give in order to receive.

These are steps to help you declutter your home.

1) If you forgot about something you own because it's been in storage or in the back of your closet... give it away.

2) If you have not worn something in over a year, let it go and bless someone else with the clothing who is currently in need.

3) Try not to get emotionally attached to belongings, because that will cause you to keep more items.

Taking care of your home is your first ministry. If you're failing at home, who cares if you're successful... What matters is who you are without the spotlight. As women, we have to take pride in the way we care for our home and place of refuge.

You live at the address of your thoughts. I can't remember where I heard that quote from, but it's so true. You literally live at the address of your thoughts. Where do you live right now? Where do you live? How did you get there? What did you think about in order to get there? I want you to realize that our homes represent a part of us. Sometimes, people live in homes that may not be very appealing or they may be embarrassed to invite people over, but at the end of the day, we live at the address of our thoughts.

Sometimes, there are people who feel like they can't maintain anything more than a section in their house. There are some people who don't want to have a home that has a big backyard, because they hate doing yard work and they don't want to cut grass. They may live in an apartment or a place that has maintenance because of how they think. They think that they don't like yards, so they don't look for a place that has a yard.

There are others that say they won't settle for anything other than a large yard, because they enjoy working outside. They enjoy gardening. You have to realize that you live in the place that you really want subconsciously. Now, I know some people are reading this thinking, 'Girl, you're crazy. I do not live here because I want to live here.' You may not want to live there, but there is something in your thought process that makes you feel that it corresponds appropriately with wherever you are in life.

If you are jobless, it may make sense to you to have a house using government assistance. That may make sense to one person. Now, there may be another person that says, 'there's no way I'm going to live on assistance. I'm going to move back home with my mamma until I save enough money or until I get a job.' Every situation is different. I'm not judging any situation. All I want you to do is look at your own. You judge your situation. You make sure that it's corresponding to where you really want to be.

Sometimes we trick ourselves into believing that we can't have something. Some people feel like they can't have that five-bedroom home. Sometimes people deceive themselves and say they'll never be a home owner. They are going to rent. They don't see themselves doing it. You have to take responsibility, because nobody has told you those things but yourself. If someone has told you what you can and cannot have and where you can and cannot live, you had a choice to believe them or not.

It goes back to you. What do you believe? You have to take responsibility. You live wherever you live because something in your mind told you that it's what you're supposed to have at that moment. If you are content with that, it's okay, but if you want to change it, do what you need to do to change it. One thing that I realize is that we live in a home and it says a lot about us and then sometimes we have a cluttered home. Sometimes people are OCD, and they have a very clean home to the point where it's not even live able because you don't want to mess anything up.

The thing is that it's your home. It's whatever you want it to be. A lot of times, people desire to have a really nice home. They feel like it has to be a big home, a large home. They start comparing their living environment with somebody else's. You have to take responsibility for what's yours. If God gave it to you, take care of it. I don't care where you are living. At one point, I told myself, 'I don't care if I'm in a hole in a wall. That hole in the wall, it's going to be mine. It's going to be clean. It's going to be nice.' At the end of the day, you make that house a home.

You have to take responsibility in making wherever you live a home until you decide to move and go somewhere else. While you're there, you have to take responsibility for that place. You need to be grateful. I remember wanting more at one point in time. I was living in a three-bedroom house. I prayed and I said that I really wanted a larger home, because we had a lot of children and I wanted a bigger house and a bigger yard. The reality was that I had to take responsibility to decide if I was ready for a bigger house.

You can't have more until you become responsible for what's given to you already, for what you currently have. You can't want a six-bedroom house if you can't take care of a three-bedroom house. I'm not saying you can't want it, but you have to be realistic with yourself. You can't want somebody to love you if you haven't loved you yet. You have to make sure that you're not giving yourself mixed signals.

Grown Woman 101

When I was preparing for a larger home, I considered everything that I wanted to complete in that three-bedroom house. In order to be ready and prepared for the house that I truly wanted, there were a lot of things that I needed to do different in that house. So, I prepared myself to move. I started de-cluttering. I started to really take pride in my home; the way I cleaned my home, the way I took care of my flowers and the yard. I told my husband what I was doing, and he was on board. There were some things that he was doing too, because our thought process was changing.

We had to prepare for a larger home, because we knew that it was going to happen, but our minds had to be right. Our minds had to be lined up with our desires. That's what we did, because you live at the address of your home. Excuse me, you live at the address of your thoughts. While we got our house under control, we were preparing to move into a larger home. It's amazing how everything happened, and it wasn't until we took responsibility for the home that we had at the time. That's what I challenge you to do.

Take responsibility for where you are now. You work on that thing. You take pride. I don't care what circumstance you are living at. It doesn't even matter. What matters is your thoughts. You don't have to stay where you are. If you want to move or if you want to do something differently, prepare yourself for that move. In the meantime, take care of what you have.

Don't forget to create your sacred space. A place special in your home where you can relax, pray, mediate, focus on your ideas, and sit in silence or with calming music.

Chapter Six: Taking Responsibility for Your Relationships

Healthy relationships are very important in your growth as a woman. To become an extraordinary woman, you have to reevaluate the relationships that you have with people often. Not everyone in your life is meant to stay there. Some people are going to be there for longer than others. We've all heard that people come in your life for a season and a reason, and some people come for a lifetime. That's so true.

The part a lot of people don't mention is that you have to know when some of these seasons are up. Oftentimes, we try to hold on to friendships and relationships with people when their season has passed, gone, shriveled up, and died. Yet you're still holding on. You have to learn to let go. You have to learn how to differentiate between when somebody is supposed to stay in your life and when it's time to release them. The thing is that it's not always easy.

A lot of times, we keep people in our lives longer than they were supposed to be there. We have to take responsibility for those friendships. If you have people in your life that take, take, take, and they add absolutely no value to your life, whose fault is that? It's your fault because you allowed them to stay there. You complain about the friend that might call you gossiping all day, but who answers those phone calls? You do. You have a choice.

You could hit ignore and send them the voicemail, or you could pick up the phone to listen to what you're dreading. It's up to you. It's all up to you. It's a choice. Taking responsibility is reminding yourself that you have a choice. People are in your life because you're aware of what it is that they are supposed to be doing in that season, or what it is you're supposed to be doing for them in that season.

One practice that a mentor of mine has shared with me is to go through everyone that you talk to daily. Go through your phone and your contacts. Mark them with plus sign if they add value to your life, or a negative or minus sign if they take from you and add absolutely no value. The next exercise is to distance yourself from the people who have a minus beside their names and add no value to your life. Love them from a distance, but let them go.

The hardest thing about this exercise is that oftentimes the people who have a minus beside their names are the people who you'd think would be the closest people to you. A lot of times, these are family members. A lot of times, these are old longtime friends. It doesn't matter who they are or what role they play in your life. If they don't add any value to your life, it's wise to love these people from a distance, because they will continue to pull from you if you allow them to.

You have to decide who do you want in your life. There are some people who complain that they don't have any friends and they want a more active social life. They want to build healthy relationships, but yet they don't give. You have to know who you are. What type of friend are you? When people invite you to events, do you go? Or do you just stay at home? And then when you plan events, you expect for everybody to show up.

You have to take responsibility and say, "My relationships with people are contingent on me, too, and how I treat them. Am I supportive? Am I a reliable friend, family member, wife, girlfriend? Am I?" You have to ask yourself those questions, because you teach people how to treat you. You absolutely do. Think about who you are to them. Are you adding to their life or are you taking from them? A relationship goes both ways. Not only friendships, but romantic relationships. You have to take responsibility for those too.

We can go on and on about how somebody did us wrong, and what our ex-husbands did and the ex-wives that he had. We go on and on about a boyfriend or your mom or your cousin. There's the blame game again, but I challenge you to look at what you contributed, too. I'm not asking you to dismiss what they've done to you. What I am asking you to do is to think about what you may have done to them. It doesn't matter what they've done to you.

Think about what you could have done. Were you available to be loved? Were you stuck on an ex? Were you still heartbroken? Were you available for them? Did you stay on social media? Are you nosy? Were you involved in other people's relationships more than your own? Think about who you are. Are you needy and clingy? Did you try to take away the person's independence to where they couldn't have a life outside of your relationship? Did you suck the life out of them?

You have to think about what it is that you have done to people. At the end of the day, that's the only thing that's going to help you to grow and have healthy relationships moving forward. You need to do that self-evaluation and take responsibility for your relationships. It takes two. Everybody has to be honest about the part that they have played.

Chapter Seven: Taking Responsibility for Your Spiritual Growth

I know this chapter may be hard for some people, and I'm going to be as loving, but as blunt as I can be, because I don't want to waste your time. However, I will tell you that a lot of people are unhappy in life because their spiritual life is not satisfactory to them. Whenever there is a disconnect spiritually, people suffer.

I don't care how much money you have, how many friends you have, or how long you've been married. All of those things that we think will make us happy will not if we aren't spiritually developed and strong. We will still experience purposeless moments in our lives where we question what it is that we are doing. We won't feel as fulfilled. We'll feel as if something is missing, and so we sometimes search and search and search, and try all of these different things in order to fill that void, when the void is spiritual.

You cannot be a fully complete person unless you tap into your spirituality and connect to the source, which is God. If I tell you anything other than what I'm telling you now, it's going to be a lie, and I am not interested in lying to anybody because I am not a liar. We've all witnessed people who are very wealthy, who have everything, or so we think. They are married, and they just seem like they have a perfect life, yet they decide to commit suicide.

There are certain things in your life that you cannot handle on your own, and you're going to need help from God. I'll be the first to tell you that having a spiritual life does not necessarily mean that you get up and go to church every Sunday. I know some people may be surprised that I just said that, considering my husband is a pastor and I'm the first lady of the church. I also know there are a lot of people who go to church, yet they are still spiritually lost and are not mature.

It's because they have not allowed themselves to be born again before God and really connect with him. These people still struggle a lot, because they have not grown. Oftentimes, they haven't been broken enough. This happens when you are at a place in life where you realize that you've tried all of these different things. You've tried drugs. You've tried money. You've tried careers. You've tried the men. You've tried all these different things. You have a baby.

You've done all these things, but yet there is still something missing. I'm telling you right now, it's God. The best way to stay or to begin a relationship with Jesus Christ is through prayer and reading God's word. I don't know if you are a Christian or not, and I'm not here to debate with you. What I am telling you is that if you feel like something is missing, you may want to evaluate where you are spiritually.

It's going to have a lot to do with the overall happiness and joy that you have in your life. An extraordinary woman recognizes that they are a spiritual being. We are spirits living in bodies. There was a you before you had a body. You must realize that there is a source and a power way beyond yourself. That's God. Recognizing that will help you become the woman that you desire to be.

I challenge you. Look at your spiritual thermometer and see, where is it? Are you hot or are you cold? God does not want us to be lukewarm. There's a saying, "Develop your relationship with God and make it personal." Going to church is important, because you are around a lot of believers. However, it can also be very dangerous, because the church is a hospital and it's full of sick people. You have to make sure that you're at a place spiritually that you can be around other sick people.

Our bodies have an immune system, and if you're really, really, really sick, you don't want to be around certain people, because you don't want to get even more sick, and you don't want to get them sick because of your immune system. It's the same thing spiritually. You have to make sure that you can take your relationship with God seriously, so that you can be around other Christians who won't make you feel worse if they are struggling. You don't want to be around people who are going to make you even sicker.

You want to be around people who are going to encourage you to grow. If you are struggling in certain areas, it's not wise to hook up with people who have the same struggles. If you know that you are a promiscuous woman, you may not want to go to church and have prayer and bible study meetings with brother so-and-so because he might be struggling with the same thing. If the two of you get together, Lord knows both of you are probably going to end up repenting later. You have to just use wisdom.

You have to make sure that you're spiritually mature enough to understand what you should be doing and what you should not be doing. There are some things that the church cannot teach you. You have to learn on your own by building your spirit up. That's praying, fasting, and reading the word of God. You can find all these things on the internet. The word of God will help you. You have to build up your spirit, because if you don't, you won't understand what's going on at church, and you can get so caught up in the routine of going to church that you will totally miss building your spirit and connecting with God on a very intimate level.

Should you go to church? The answer is absolutely. It's important to be around believers. However, you have to make sure that your desire to grow and connect with God on intimate, individual, and personal level is more important. You just have to make sure that you prioritize your growing, and that you're not just going. You've heard me use this phrase several times in the book, 'don't go through it, grow through it.' Make sure that you're positioning yourself to grow spiritually. Find a quiet place in your home to relax and mediate. Meditate on the things you are grateful for. Think about the peace that you desire and welcome into your life. Ask God to speak to your heart. Meditation also allows my spirit to be ministered to by the Holy Spirit. If you are in need on direction, peace, or a stronger connection with God, meditation will get you there.

You can have everything that you've ever wanted, but without God, none of it has any meaning.

Chapter Eight: Taking Responsibility for Your Career

If you're like most people, you'll spend the majority of your life working. It's disappointing to go to college and enter into the workforce, only to discover that you hate your career. Someone has lied to us. What's popular in the American culture has failed us. We have been programmed from an early age to get an education, get a job, make money, and be happy. In reality you'll find that it's the least happy people who have followed this model.

No one dares to dream anymore. Who would you truly become if money and fear weren't an issue? Are you willing to find out? Most of us will never reach our greatest potential due to fear, rejection, and approval-seeking from friends and family. What do you enjoy doing for free? Think about it! What brings you great joy and has absolutely nothing to do with money? Your passion needs you. No one can do the things that you were designed to do, but you. Don't die with your passion and your dreams.

It's not uncommon to experience a lack of support from those who are closet to you. In fact, we have all experienced it at some point in our careers. When you started your business endeavors, you were excited and wanted your loved ones to be excited as well. It doesn't take long to realize who is truly there to cheer you on. This can be very difficult to accept. The disappointment of a lack of support can become extremely overwhelming. So what do you do?

Once you have discovered who your non-supportive family and friends are, it can be challenging to prevent this from affecting your relationship with them. Being around them can feel dreadfully awkward. When you are passionate about your career, it's easy to take offense when others don't understand your vison. Avoiding these people may seem like the easiest solution, however, it may further strain the relationship. I know some of us cut off relationships rather quickly, instead of revaluating where we have placed these people in our lives. The reality is that not all of your family and friends are going to become your customers, clients, or biggest fans.

Promoting to a warm market may be okay for some people, but don't forget that business is business. Identify your target market and spend your energy there. If some of your loved ones have been identified as your targeted market, remember that they still have options and are not obligated to do business with you. Either way, respect their decision. Mixing business and personal relationships can be far more damaging than a lack of support, especially if money is involved.

Entrepreneurs are a rare breed, and you cannot expect everyone to understand your way of thinking. Misunderstandings could also be interpreted as rejection. If someone chooses not to support you and your endeavors, I encourage you to not take it personally. You must always consider the source. The background of the source is critical. If you're doing something that they're unable to do themselves, oftentimes they will assume that you cannot do it either. When it comes to business, surround yourself with likeminded people. Discuss business topics with business-savvy people. They can appreciate your creativity and what you have to offer. With the time that you spend trying to convince people to believe in you, you could instead be rerouting that energy towards evolving in your field.

I have come to understand that people are in your life for different reasons. I have certain friends and family members that I can discuss business with, whereas I may share another aspect of my life with other ones, such as spirituality, family, entertainment, etc. Your life will go much more smoothly once you categorize everyone appropriately. However, after doing so, you may realize that some people have no place in your life. Those are the people that you want to reconsider having in your circle of influence. Everyone in our life has a role to play, and not everyone's role is going to involve your business. Please remember, this does not mean that they do not love you.

Staying Focused

There are countless distractions throughout the day, but staying focused is possible. We all have busy lives, and sometimes we feel crazy trying to juggle so many tasks. Multi-tasking is second nature for most women, but it can also become our worst enemy. It can cause you to stretch yourself so thin that it makes it difficult to notice any progress from your efforts. We may find ourselves working, working, working, but nothing has changed other than our stress levels. Yes! As your stress increases, you adapt to it as your new normal. Stress becomes your way of life, and so do your bad habits of creating distractions.

After coaching many clients about their career goals, lack of focus is among the most common road blocks that stand in their path to success. Have you ever wondered how some people accomplish so much with their time? I use to ask myself that question all the time. Then it dawned on me that all of us have 24 hours in a day. It wasn't that I was wasting my time, I was merely mismanaging it. That means that I was doing a little bit of a lot every day. Gosh, was I wrong. I had no idea that I'd actually be more productive if I focused on one task at a time. That should have been a no brainer, right? Not for women who are used to multitasking incorrectly. If you give your energy and undivided attention to one task at a time, you might notice a difference in what you're able to accomplish every day. Of course, I'm not suggesting that you discontinue doing multiple things. However, it wouldn't hurt to do one of those things for an extended period of time.

If you're struggling with staying focused, here are some things that I'd encourage you to try.

- **Plan Your Day-** In order to do this properly, ask yourself, "What are the things that I absolutely must accomplish in order to feel satisfied and productive?"
- **Prioritize-** Consider putting the things that you dread doing at the top of your list of things to do. Oftentimes, this eliminates or decreases procrastination.
- **Main Focus-** Decide what you'd like to spend the majority of your time doing, instead of multitasking everything. Choose one thing or project to give your undivided attention to.

Consider spending 2 - 4 hours on your main focus.

- **<u>Limit Distractions-</u>** Distractions are everywhere, however becoming disciplined in this area could potentially free up several hours of your day. Email, personal phone calls, Facebook, television, and other guilty pleasures could be costing you crucial time. And for most of us, time is money.

The strategies mentioned may not be for your line of work, but they are intended to be used as a guide in implementing whatever is useful for your particular purpose. Stay focused, and you will be on your way to becoming the best you. Stay focused, distractions are everywhere! However, God has a plan that needs your undivided attention. Are you listening for His divine direction? Your purpose is attached to your passion.

Quotes for the Boss Ladies:

SET SOME GOALS, THEN DEMOLISH THEM

Instagram Sheconquers

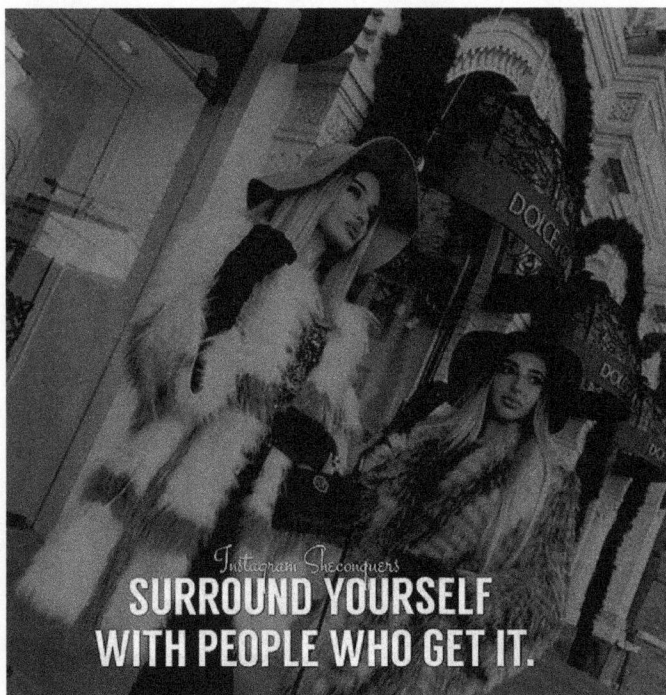

SURROUND YOURSELF
WITH PEOPLE WHO GET IT.

DON'T JUDGE ME UNTIL YOU KNOW ME, DON'T UNDERESTIMATE ME UNTIL YOU CHALLENGE ME, DON'T TALK ABOUT ME UNTIL YOU'VE TALKED TO ME.

MADE BY
THEGOODVIBE.CO

thegoodquote.co

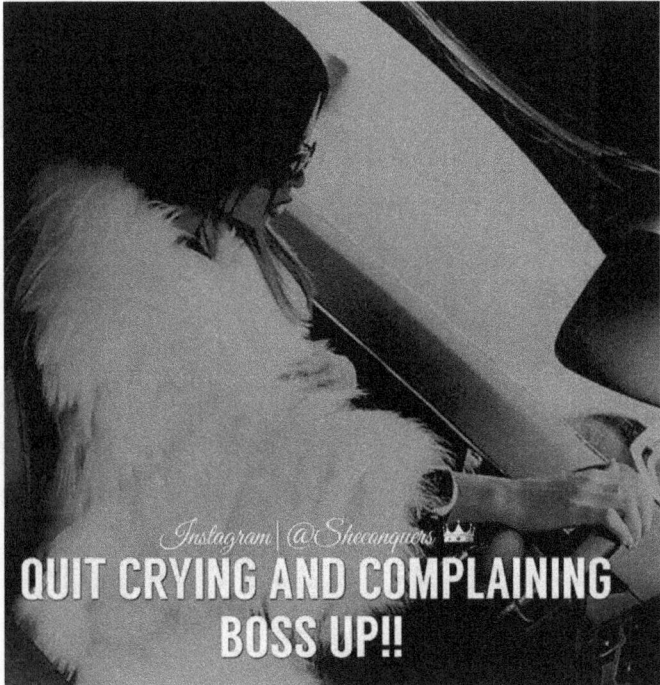

Instagram | @Sheconquers

QUIT CRYING AND COMPLAINING
BOSS UP!!

Every next level of your life
will demand a different you.

LOOK IN THE
MIRROR...
THAT'S YOUR
COMPETITION.

**GRIND
WHILE THEY SLEEP.
LEARN
WHILE THEY PARTY.
LIVE
LIKE THEY DREAM.**

secrets2success

A *Successful*
woman
Is one
who can **build**
a firm foundation
with the
Bricks others
have THROWN at her

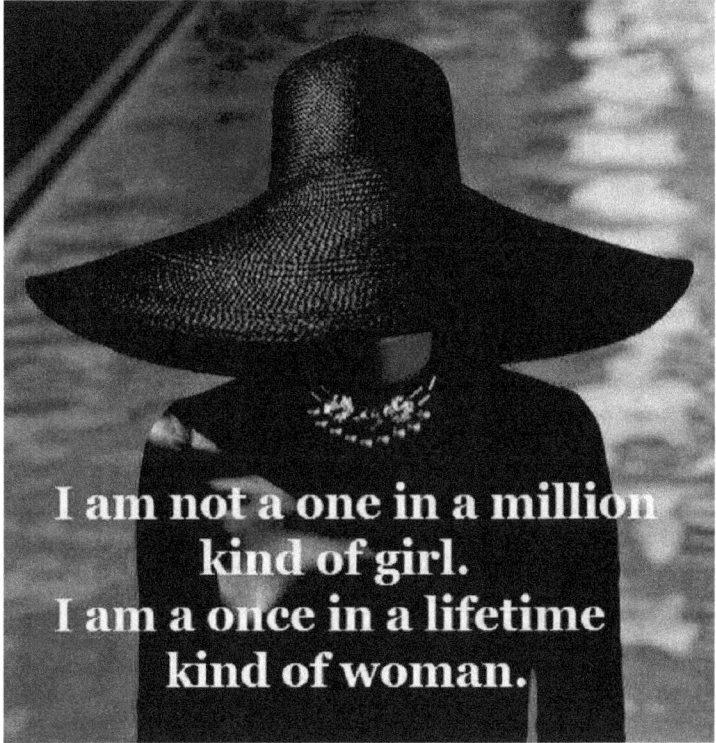

I am not a one in a million
kind of girl.
I am a once in a lifetime
kind of woman.

PICTUREQU♥TES. com

MOST WOMEN WANT A MAN THAT'S ALREADY ESTABLISHED. A STRONG WOMAN WILL BE A PART OF HIS STRUGGLE, SURVIVE IT, SUCCEED TOGETHER, AND BUILD AN EMPIRE.

Strong women don't play victim, don't make themselves look pitiful, & don't point fingers. They stand & they deal.

Mandy Hale

DON'T
WAIT
until you've
reached your goal
to be proud of yourself.
BE PROUD OF
every step you take toward
reaching your goal.

"People who shine from within don't need the spotlight."

Instagram | Fitxlyfe

A MISTAKE REPEATED MORE THAN ONCE IS A DECISION.

Chapter Nine: Taking Responsibility for Your Goals

There are certain things in life that you may desire to do. Setting goals are fantastic, however, do you have the discipline to reach them? The first thing you have to do is ask yourself, 'have I truly committed to this goal? Or am I just talking?' You cannot get upset if you don't reach your goal if you haven't realistically done anything to accomplish it. A lot of times, people use smart goals. A smart goal is a goal that's specific, measurable, obtainable, realistic and time-able. For example, a smart goal would be something like, "I want to lose 10 pounds within the next 30 days."

The reason why it's a smart goal is because it's specific; you're saying how much weight you want to lose. It's time-able, you're saying exactly how much time you have to do it. It's measurable. You're giving yourself 30 days, so at the end of those 30 days you can measure and see if you've reached that goal, or if you fell short from it. It has to be obtainable. And it is. That's realistic. Some people can lose 10 pounds in 30 days, right? You just want to make sure that it meets the criteria. That's what a smart goal is.

If you have commitment issues and you procrastinate, then reaching your goals may be very hard. You have to commit to them. You have to be faithful to you. If you're not faithful to yourself, you can't expect other people to be faithful to you. A lot of people cheat on their diets. You have to form a good relationship with yourself and where you want to be. It's the you now compared to the you then. Now and then. Now and then. Now and later.

You have to make sure that you're keeping your promises to that person 30 days from now, that's going to be yourself, just essentially 10 pounds lighter. If you don't keep your commitment to yourself within 30 days, then you are lying to yourself over and over and over again, and your goals don't mean anything. You make goals all the time that are not realistic, and you're not going to achieve them. Then you will never take anything that you want to do in life seriously. How do you change this bad habit of not keeping your promises and reaching your goals? You start with one goal at a time.

Choose one area that you would like to create a goal in. It could be any area in your life. Whatever that goal is, I want you to create a smart goal. I want you to stick with it until you accomplish it. Once you accomplish that, you can go on to the next thing. You have to take responsibility for your goals. Nobody can reach that goal for you, but yourself. One thing I do to help me with my goals is to create a vision board. A vision board is basically a poster board. I'll cut out different things from magazines to represent my goal.

I'll also cut out words, pictures, and things of that nature. It helps to have a visual reminder of your goal. I have mine posted up in my office, and I make them often. I'm looking at my vision board right now, and I have about three poster boards up there. Some things have come to pass. Some things I'm still working on. It's important to have your vision board, but it's not only significant for you to have a vision board, but it's very appropriate to close your eyes and imagine those things happening.

Close your eyes and imagine yourself 10 pounds lighter. Imagine yourself actually in the store shopping for new clothes because you went down a size or two. It has to be realistic to you. If it's not realistic to you, then you're probably not going to follow through with it. You have to see yourself taking pictures and selfies and telling all your friends that you lost 10 pounds. You have to get excited. You have to build up the moment and it has to be real to you. Not the goal, but the end result.

The end result has to be real to you. It has to be so real to you that you feel it. You're looking in your closet and you're seeing the new size that you wear, you see the new jeans, you have to see it in order to believe it. See it in your mind, put it on a vision board, and commit to it, and that is the path that's going to change all your bad habits to help you accomplish the goals that you really want to reach. The journey is tough, but the view from the top is worth it. You are worth it! A lot of people are getting older, but not growing up and putting on their big girl panties. In order to reach your goals, you have to make changes instead of excuses. Your life is a reflection of your thoughts, decisions, and mindset.

When you choose to follow your dreams, people will think that you're crazy, because they are afraid to follow theirs. Don't be afraid to dream. What people think of you is absolutely none of your business. Let their negative thoughts remain in their space. You don't have to take it. Surround yourself with people that believe in you. Sometimes, that may even make you a loner. Life is about taking risks, also known as having faith. All you need is enough light for the step that you're on. You don't need to see the entire staircase. Most of us would end up procrastinating out of doubt and fear anyway. Just focus on each step. Small steps over time amount to huge accomplishments later. Stay positive, your goal is dependent on it.

Chapter Ten: Taking Responsibility for Your Past

Have you ever looked back at your past and been embarrassed or ashamed of something you've done or been through? I think many of us have had past experiences, things that we've done or said, and people that we've associated with that we are not proud of, but in order to grow you have to take responsibility for everything in your past that has happened.

In the beginning of the book, I mentioned a couple of scenarios, but there are times when we just don't want to talk about our past. It doesn't matter what these are, as long as you find peace and are taking responsibility so that you can move on, because if you're reliving your past often and you're thinking about the mistakes that you've made or the people you've hurt or the people who have hurt you, that means there is no peace there.

Once you make peace with your past, you're able to move on without the feelings of guilt, shame, rejection, and abandonment. Whatever your past issues, you can be free from them once you make peace with them. For me, making peace with my past was just realizing that I had a responsibility to make sure I had an accurate perspective on my past.

I made a lot of mistakes when I was younger, and so to change the perspective I had on my past in order to find peace was to look at it in the most mature way that I could. I realized that my past was nothing more than my life learning experiences, that have transformed me and now allow me to help thousands of women get through things, because I have similar experiences in various areas of my life.

Not everything that I went through was all bad. It gave me the credentials to be able to speak on a lot of the topics that I'm able to teach today. I ask that you go back into your past and change your perspective. If you had a relationship that was awful, what did you learn from it? You may have learned that you really don't like to be treated that way, or you may have learned that you really don't like that type of people or person, but you always learn something about yourself. You have to take responsibility for who your past has transformed you into.

It wasn't in vain. It's all a part of your story. It's all a part of what makes you who you are. It doesn't define you, but it definitely helps to shape you and to mold you into the woman that you are now, that you are becoming. I ask that you go back and think about your past, make peace with your past, and determine how you can take responsibility for the perspective you have on your past in order to move on and use your past as your stepping stone to take you to the next level.

It's essential to learn how to live in the present moment. Choosing to remain in the past is simply choosing to opt out of the day. That's correct! You're actually robbing yourself from days, weeks, or maybe even years. Life will go on, with or without you. Grown women understand that you cannot go back in time. However, you can use the past to your advantage. Your past is your book of lessons, knowledge, experience, and stepping stones. We all have a past, but I'd like to invite you to enjoy life in the current and present moment.

I use to be stuck in my past. I would relive past failures, hurt, and even my accomplishments, over and over again. My false sense of reality was preventing me from moving forward. I was stuck. I was so busy looking back, that I hadn't realized that my thought process was actually hindering me. I was walking backwards into my future. What happens when you walk backwards? In my experience, I move more slowly and run the risk of bumping into something. It's uncomfortable and unnatural. Walking backwards also took away my vision. I was only focused on what I could see: my past.

Grown Woman 101

There comes a time in your life, when you make a decision to turn around and walk forward towards your future. You will go much further and have fewer distractions once you can see where you're going. You will get excited and see things that were not obvious before. Today is a new day. Choose to walk forward.

Taking Responsibility for Your Happiness

How to Encourage Yourself

Life can be overwhelming sometimes, and you might fall into depression if you lack daily encouragement. It's easier to stay encouraged than to pull yourself out from depression. Most of us agree that preventative maintenance is better than digging yourself out from a state of depression or discouragement. There are many benefits to having a positive attitude and being encouraged, especially when you're experiencing hard times. Lack of encouragement can cause some women to feel rejected, insignificant, and underappreciated. I must inform you that if you're seeking outside validation, then you may become disappointed every time. You have to search within yourself and pull out that inner strength from knowing your worth and value. It's dangerous to sit around and wait for other people to affirm you. What if no one takes the time to encourage you? When you chose to hand over that control to someone else, your happiness is placed in the palm of their hand, and you become the victim if they fail to meet your expectations.

Encouraging yourself will take some practice. You must learn to cancel out your negative thoughts with an abundance of positive thoughts towards yourself. Your mind and thoughts can become your worst enemy, and it will take some work to lead your mind and not follow your negative thoughts. Here are some tips to practice self-encouragement.

- Do not trust your feelings - sometimes your emotions can and will deceive you.
- Focus on your assets and not your shortcomings.
- Surround yourself with positive people.
- When receiving advice, ALWAYS consider the source.
- Don't ignore compliments; write down the compliments that people give you.
- Whenever you get discouraged, refer to your compliment notes.

Writing your compliments down could literally become a life saver. There may be many times in life when you become too weak mentally, emotionally, or spiritually to encourage yourself. If this ever happens, your book of compliments can offer you the encouragement that you need. I have personally referred to my book of compliments during really tough times in my life. During my first book signing, I passed around a notebook and asked my guest to write down words of encouragement for me. I had no idea how important that book would become when I found myself battling depression years later. You may hear people telling you to encourage yourself, and it almost becomes a cliché, but it's not. Encouraging yourself will give you the opportunity to live your life in a different perspective. You can embrace your life for the lessons that it offers, the ability to see yourself in a brighter light, and opportunity to love yourself completely.

If you have the desire to see yourself differently, then you just have to start seeing yourself differently. It may take some time, but you can do it! Writing out all of your personal strengths and flaws will allow you to realize how you truly see yourself. Look at the flaws, and realize what you can improve and what you have no control over. Commit to a small goal in the areas where you can make some changes to improve whatever it is that you are not satisfied with. For the things that you cannot change, write down a more positive way of viewing that area of your life. The way you see yourself is only a reflection of your thoughts.

It's not anyone's responsibility to make you happy. That's giving another person too much power over your life. They can make you happy, but then they also have the power to make you unhappy. It's not wise to hand someone the key to your happiness. Protect your happiness by realizing that it comes from within. No one can take what's inside of you unless you give it away.

Chapter Eleven: Taking Responsibility for Being Stuck

Are You a Slave to Your Past?

Liberty is often associated with freedom, yet few people have ever experienced it. Although you may not be physically bound and restricted, you could still be holding yourself hostage. We all have a past, and you may be one of those people who has experienced a lot of hurt and pain that could be preventing you from moving forward in your life today. The past is difficult to deal with, so many of us choose to allow it to lay dormant and ignored. Coping with life is not the same as living life. One cannot live an abundant life until you have confronted the past and applied the chapters that are attached to it. The past is there to offer you nuggets of life, chapters, and pearls of wisdom, if you chose to accept it as such.

The past can have a lot of power over your present life if you fail to acknowledge it. Ignoring your past could become the elephant in the room if it involves a multitude of hurt feelings. The past should be considerate as exactly that, "the past". Oftentimes, we merge the past into our present, and it takes away from the potential of our future. This can be true with past successes as well. Reliving your past accomplishments and dwelling on them can rob you of the chance to move forward, make new goals, and form new, creative ideas.

Past events should be your motivation to do and want something better and greater. This is true for both positive and negative events that have occurred. Turn the negative events into a positive life chapters, and use the positive events as a stepping stone to reach greater heights. Your past is what you make of it. If you allow it to hold you captive, it most certainly will. However, if you give yourself permission to grow from it, you'll be surprised as to who you can become with the experiences that you were given.

Choosing to acknowledge the past for what it is, can open your eyes to a whole new level of thinking and possibilities. What if you became the mother that you never had or mentored other hurting people who are currently going through what you have already survived? Your past is another person's hope. Your past is the key to your future, and the amount of influence that you could have in this world. Do not continue to pour salt in your own wounds if you are still hurting from an offense from your past. Give yourself permission to heal, so that you can begin a new chapter in your life. Turn the page and discover what is waiting for you. It's never too late to become who you have been called to be. There is liberty in celebrating who you are today and the possibilities of tomorrow. Live beyond your past, because those who live in their past are no longer living in reality. Life will go on, with or without you. Choose to participate, choose to be free.

Chapter Twelve: Taking Responsibility for Your Failures

I want to first remind you, and if you've never heard this I want to be the first to tell you, that failure is an event, not a person. You're not a failure, although we have failures that sometimes occur in our life, but they aren't only failures, they are opportunities to get it right. It's often hard to do something right if you've never done it wrong before. Look at every area in your life where you feel like you've failed, and use it as an opportunity to correct it, to make it better.

There are some things you may not chronologically be able to go back and make better. However, it will either give you the opportunity to help someone else, or you may have an opportunity to go back and make it right. What does that mean? I know there are a lot of parents that feel like they failed as a parent and they didn't do what they needed to do, and so what will happen is that they will then overcompensate with how they treat their grandchildren.

Have you guys ever noticed that grandchildren are treated a lot differently than how their parents were treated? I've witnessed it even in my own family. There are certain things that my mother would do for my children that I know for a fact she did not do for me when I was younger, but a lot of times, those grandparents will identify areas in their life where they may have missed the mark. Maybe they worked too much and they weren't there as often as they could have been for their own children, and so they try to do things differently with their grandchildren.

Although they can't change what happened and how they raised their own kids, they have an opportunity to do things differently as a grandparent. Or you may have the opportunity to go back and talk to your children and apologize to your children, because a grown woman knows how to take responsibility when she missed the mark.

You're not prideful and you can humble yourself and say, you know, I really didn't do a good job at this, or I really didn't do a good job at that, and it's not about someone accepting your apology, but sometimes you just need to give in, because a truly grown woman knows how to ask for forgiveness, and she also knows how to forgive even when someone does not ask for it.

There are areas in your life that you may feel like you've just failed. Lord knows, I feel like there are so many things that I've failed at in life. What did you learn from those times, and how can you make it right? I have countless things that I've felt like I failed at, but you have another day to make it right.

You have another day to make different decisions and to not take those days for granted. Remember that a failure is an event. It's not a person. You're not a person. You can have a failure and not be a failure. Think about how all of your failures in life can be changed for your benefit. How can you make those things right, and how can you do things differently?

STANDARDS

GROWN WOMEN ALWAYS HAVE HIGH STANDARDS

Chapter Thirteen: Setting Standards

It's important for you to set standards for yourself. Others may have standards for you, and that's great, but not good enough. Sometimes, your pastor has standards for you, or your parents have standards for you (or did when you were younger). Your children, they have standards for you. Your husband may have standards for you. None of that matters unless you have standards for yourself. What are your standards? Do you even know? What are the boundaries that you have? Do you know? You have to learn who you are and what standards you believe exist in your life today. Setting standards in your life is crucial to becoming the kind of warrior woman that you are.

There are some women out there that are single and have been for years, and so they'll settle and date a married man. They'll tell themselves lies in order to excuse their behavior, and say, "Well, he is separated," or "they're not happy," or "he's leaving his wife." They believe these lies to excuse their behavior. The reality is, a married man ,is a married man, is a married man, and I don't care if they're separated or what other circumstances there may be. I don't care if he is waiting on a divorce. He is not married to you.

If you don't know how to differentiate between a single man and a married man, ask the IRS. How does he file his taxes, single or married? Because they don't ask if you are separated, but that's just a defense mechanism that some women will use so that they don't have to take responsibility for their lack of standards and sleeping with someone else's husband.

I don't want you guys to think that I'm being judgmental. I'm just sharing the facts, and you have to look at yourself and you have to realize what's true and what's a false perception that you've given yourself in order to make yourself feel good. Now, a grown woman doesn't want a false illusion to make her feel good. You want to live in reality and you want to live in truth, and so you have to make sure that your standards are aligned with the woman that you desire to be.

If you're okay with being a mistress, then you have to be real about your standards. If you desire to be a wife, you have to raise the bar and say, "Well, I can't be a wife to somebody else's husband." You have to be realistic about the standards that you're setting for yourself. Now I just used that scenario as an example, but there are so many different examples of setting standards for yourself.

Sometimes, this could happen on a job where you're settling for one position, when you know in your heart that you could work other positions, but because you're

Grown Woman 101

scared of failing, you just take a mediocre position and excel at that, instead of continuing to advance and challenge yourself and learn new skills. Then again, you have set a standard for yourself in the work place. That standard is, "I'm just going to stay where I'm comfortable, and I don't want to do anything else because I don't want to fail."

That's a standard that you've set for yourself. Whereas there maybe somebody else who takes opportunities left and right because their standard is, "I don't have a bar or a glass ceiling above my head. I want to keep moving up and up until I can't move up any more, but I'm going to try and I'm going to take every opportunity that comes my way." I remember somebody shared with my husband the meaning of being poor, and they said it meant that they passed over opportunities repeatedly.

If you think about it, that's true. For somebody that has passed over opportunities repeatedly, that's the standard that they've set for themselves. The standard is, "I'm not going to go after another opportunity because I'm fearful, so therefore I'm going to complain about where I'm at," but then again, they're not doing anything to change their situation. That's a standard that the people have set for themselves. Ask yourself.

Think about a few standards that you have in your life. What are your standards for finances? What are your

Grown Woman 101

standards for your career? What are your standards for friendships? What are standards for spiritual growth? What are your standards for relationships? What are your standards for your time? How are you spending your time? What are your standards, because if you don't know, that means that you're just going to blow with the wind.

You have to know what your standards are. You have to know what your boundaries are, because if you don't know, then you're not taking responsibility, you're just going with the flow. A grown woman is not going to go with the flow. You have to be confident in what you want, where you are, and where you are going. A confident woman knows that she has to be a woman of standards.

Chapter Fourteen: Standards for Life

Setting standards overall is great, but in order to set a standard for your life, you need to be honest about what you want out of your life. Setting a standard for your life may require you to prioritize what matters most to you. Is it your family? Is it your job? Is it your spiritual growth? Is it your money, your time? You have to figure out what is it that you truly want, and where it falls within your life.

Standards for your life will help you become happy, because a lot of times, people are unhappy because they really don't know what they want in life. Some people say they want a career, and they go after the career only to realize that they really wanted to be a wife, because they never sat down with themselves and set their overall standard for life and what they truly desired and were honest about it.

People become depressed and miserable essentially, and so you have to ask, what is it that you want? What are your standards for living? When I realized that I didn't have any standards for life, I knew that was why my life was all over the place. I wanted to do everything and be everyone, and what I mean by that is, the house, the wife, the kids, the career, the church, I just wanted it all, but I didn't know how to prioritize any of that.

My life had no standards, so it was everywhere. Then it became a point in time where I realized, yeah, I do want all of these things, but I have to figure out what's most important, and I began to prioritize my life, readjusted some things, and made my spiritual life the most important thing to me, because I felt like if I wasn't strong spiritually, then everything else in my life wouldn't matter. When I began to strengthen my spiritual life, God started to show me where to place everything else after that.

My standard for life was to strengthen my spiritual life first and believe that everything else would be put in its proper position and respective place and I trusted that, and that's what happened for me. In order to have those standards for your life, you have to know what your purpose is overall. My standard for my life was that I did not want to live another day without pursuing my purpose.

I encourage you to take a moment and think about what your standard for life is. What do you want from it? What's your purpose for being here? What's your purpose for reading this book? An extraordinary woman knows the standard of life that she has is what she wants, what she needs, and what makes her uniquely her.

Chapter Fifteen: Standards for Your Inner Circle

Be Selective

It's important to be very selective who you let into your inner circle. Typically, this consists of your closest friends, and it's true that birds of a feather flock together. Your friends have some type of common core compatibility with you, and that's why you're so close. Your friends are a representation of a part of you. If you think about it, you have a common ground with them. Statistically, it's shown that you make within $2,000 of your closest four friends. Look at your four closest friends, and statistics show that you make within $2,000 of what your friends are making. I know a lot of people say, "I want to be a millionaire." My first response is that you're going to need to find some millionaire friends, because you are a reflection of the company you keep. If you're around negative people, you are going to eventually start thinking very negatively and doubt yourself. If you're around gossipers, chances are you're gossiping with them.

If you don't like those types of people or if you don't want to be that type of person, you have to find a different caliber of people who represent where you want to go so that you can learn from them. If your friends are not helping you grow and they're not meeting the life standards that you feel you've set for yourself, then it may be time to just move them to another category. I'm not saying to get rid of your friends, but you have to reposition them. This is okay and it's necessary, as we learned in the earlier chapters.

I want you to take responsibility for your inner circle of friends. They are there because you allow them to still be there. You grant them that access to your inner circle, which is the closest part of your immediate nuclear family, and you gave them access to you. You have to be very selective with who you allow to be connected to you, because you reflect each other. If you see things in your friends that you don't like, I want you to then examine yourself and see why is it that this person is as close to you as they are, and why you dislike as many of the things about them as you do, yet you don't want to become like them, and yet you stay connected.

I need you to evaluate those relationships with your inner circle. Take responsibility and decide to keep them or decide to reposition them, because they will affect you. Show me your friends, and I'll show you your future.

By default, your circle will likely look like this.

As you become more confident in life, you'll begin to rearrange the people in your life. It's common to have family members who were once close to you by default, but eventually moved further out of your circle because you had the choice to allow only healthy relationships near you. Look at this diagram, and decide if the right people are in the proper position to compliment who you are becoming.

Your life starts out looking like this; however, you have the power to rearrange your social circle as you grow and evolve. Some people may stay in their original position, but don't be surprised when you have to move the closest people further out and away from you.

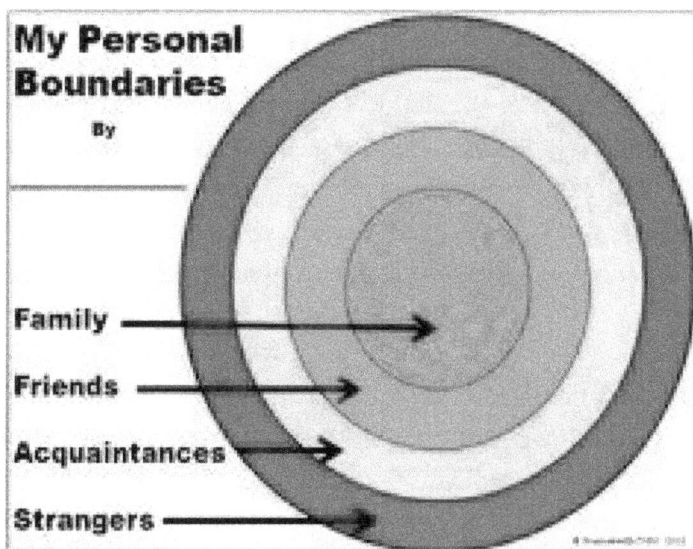

My Personal Boundaries

By

Family

Friends

Acquaintances

Strangers

Chapter Sixteen: Standards for Your Emotion

As women, we are very emotional, but you have to understand how to have standards for your emotions and what that means exactly. Even your emotions need boundaries. A grown woman cannot afford to be emotionally unbalanced, under developed, and immature. It's okay to be vulnerable, but you have to know when to cry, when to smile, when to love, and when to cut people out of your life. It is hardest to differentiate the emotions from our adult selves and those from our childhood state. You cannot expect to operate on a grown woman's level when you allow your inner child to control you emotionally. Give yourself permission to grow up.

You have to know when to grieve and do all of these other things, and it's so confusing because with female hormones, we can have five different emotions within five minutes, but you have to become responsible for your emotions. The type of emotions that I'm referring to right now are insecurity and jealousy. The things that we like, we can't control because people have done us wrong, so we don't trust anyone and we always think somebody is cheating on us.

You can't have any healthy relationships with your friends because you're jealous in your ambiance. If this is you, you need to really check your emotions and set some standards. How do you set standards? If you're a jealous person, you have to look at yourself and think about all that you have to offer and stop looking at other people, because when you compare yourself, you know it makes you feel bad. Stop comparing yourself to people.

People should like you for who you are. You don't have to compare yourself to anybody. There is only one you and there is only one them, so you really can't compare anyway, but when we try to do it, a lot of times we fall short. You cannot compare yourself to other people. If you know that you're insecure, you know that you're a jealous person and you know that you can't trust anybody, and that's why you say, "I don't deal with women, and I don't have female friends."

You say all this just because you don't trust them, and so you have to be honest with yourself and ask what that reason is. Why don't you have female friends? Why don't you get along with anybody? Why are you so insecure? A lot of times, that will go back to our past, and as we learned in an earlier chapter, we need to make peace with our past. Has a woman done something to make you not trust her? Has a man done something to you to make you insecure?

You have to set some standards for your emotions or they're going to be all over the place, because you don't tell your emotions how to feel. You set standards and you raise the bar so that your emotions can catch up. What does that mean? You have to build your confidence up so much that your emotions no longer have control over you, but you tell your emotions how to feel instead.

You can see a woman who is attractive and not feel intimidated by her, because your standards are, "I'm a beautiful woman. Yeah, that woman she is nice looking, she can dress, she is intelligent. I'm not worried about my man looking at her because I know I'm bad, I'm beautiful, and I know I'm attractive also."

Men are attracted to confidence. If you're all over the place and you're accusing him of looking at somebody, then you're just insecure, you're jealous; you are pushing him into the arms of somebody else, because nobody wants to deal with that for a long period of time. If you are in a relationship and he hasn't gone anywhere, he may not be the happiest if you have your emotions all over the place. You have to get those emotions in check so that you don't lose your mind and you don't drive the people around you crazy.

Do a favor for them as well as for yourself. Set some standards for your emotions and practice growing up. There are a whole lot of chronologically grown women, but they're really little girls. There are a lot of men who don't know how to conduct themselves with women. They don't know how to be in a room with other beautiful women without feeling intimidated. There are a lot of women that call themselves women, but they're catty. They don't even know how to build another sister up.

They're always tearing other people down, because they don't understand the power of lifting somebody up and what that means - encouraging and inspiring that other person. They don't understand what it means to be around other successful women without feeling like they're a failure. Don't be that woman. Set some emotional standards for yourself.

Whoever it is that you want to be, you can be her, but you've got to let that little girl grow up. Think about where you are emotionally and what areas you need to improve on, and dedicate time to setting some goals and reaching the goals emotionally, and setting those standards so that you can be the extraordinary woman that you desire to be.

A grown woman also takes the high road. A woman who knows when to be quiet and when to speak is a powerful woman. If you're talking a mile a minute and have no substance, you're speaking foolishly. If you only open your mouth to speak when you truly have something to say, people with listen. Grown Women speak with wisdom. There's no need to argue to make your point clear. Communication is key, along with tone, and a tamed tongue shows a woman's maturity level.

Don't get emotional when people don't like or understand you. In fact, expect some controversy. Immature women think that you're taking their light, while in reality, your light doesn't take away from anyone else's. You don't need someone's light to shine; you were born with your own. Please remember that you don't need anyone's approval to be awesome. Never apologize for being great, even if it offends insecure people.

The Fight

I didn't know how much courage it actually took to LIVE until I found myself wanting to die. I wanted to kill myself because the pain that I had experienced in life was too unbearable to deal with. I had lived a large portion of my life trying to please others; whenever I let my spectators down, I felt like a failure. I had no idea how to truly think for myself. Growing up as a "PK," aka a preacher's kid, I felt like I was not able to make mistakes. However no one is perfect. The more mistakes I made, and the more I tried to cover them up, the more I was creating pain deep down inside of me. My life became a lie, and I no longer knew who I was. I had always been defined by my association with others. My father was a preacher, so I guess I was a good church girl; my brother was a drug dealer, so I guess I was a girl next door hood chick; because of my beautiful, sophisticated mother, I guess I was supposed to be educated and successful. I was married, and with that came a different family and even a different last name, only to find myself feeling abandoned when the marriage ended. As I got older, I had associations from my own life that also seemed to define me. I got to a point in my life where I felt smothered by everyone's opinions of me and what they thought that I should be doing with my life. I soon realized that if you allow others to plan your life for you…. THEY WILL. I also learned that whenever you reject their directions, opinions, and advice, you could consequently become their enemy simply because you won't give them the power to influence or control your life. Trying to control others is a form of witchcraft; I didn't fully believe that until I felt obligated to fulfill the opinions of others. I was weak and held hostage to the judgments of many people in my life. I couldn't breathe. Then, I decided take a chance and live my life for me, to have God direct me and no one else. That sounds great right? But it all came with a cost; I had to have the "Courage to Live."

Many of you may know how it feels to fight for your life. If you understand that struggle, then this book will definitely bless you. For the rest of you who have never had to endure such adversity, you will gain a better understanding about those of us who know this story all too well. It's crazy, because I never knew that I was fighting for my life until the fight was over. I'm not referring to a physical, tangible fight, but more like a mental and spiritual fight. I sometimes get angry when I think about everything that contributed to my struggle. Some of the things I could have prevented but wasn't strong enough to resist. Other things I had no control over and had to endure the pain. All of these struggles would inevitably make me who I am today. The fight was similar to someone drowning, just trying to keep her head above water. Spiritually I was drowning. I was burnt out, tired, weak, and ready to throw in the towel. I had no more fight in me, and that's right where God wanted me to be.

My fight started when I was seventeen. Being a senior in high school and pregnant wasn't my ideal life, but I tried to make the best of it. Trying to make my obvious sin disappear, I agreed to marry the father. Somehow, I thought that I'd turn away the heads of the people who judged me. It's funny now, because all I did was create more attention on my situation. Unfortunately, teen pregnancy is common, but being married at the age of seventeen is a hot mess. I was deceived to think that I'd taken the attention off of me, not realizing that I had added to it. I wanted life to be great but had no idea what that "great life" was supposed to entail. My plans always seemed to fail; of course, I was not seeking any guidance from God. A lot of you have heard my story already, and I don't want to bore you with the details. That segment of my life was an ingredient used by the enemy to fuel my insecurities. It started a bad habit: I thought that I was in control of my life and that the people around me knew what was best for me. The only problem was that they were all human.

This book is not meant to focus on my pain but on how I decided to have the courage to live and not just exist. I no longer wanted to feel like a victim or to play the role of a victim. I was not the only person that had to live through various trials, and I was tired of throwing myself a pity party. I had a few questions that I needed to ask myself: What did my past teach me? What did I learn about myself and others? Well, the answers were obvious. I learned through my pain that I was a fighter. I learned that I was a lot stronger than I gave myself credit for. I learned that people are still people, and I learned that I could not afford to be spiritually weak.

The fight for my life started when I learned how weak I was. In order to fight, I had to become stronger spiritually. I had a relationship with God, but I still had to be roughed up and toughened up a bit more. God was strengthening me so that I could endure hard times. When you think about a boxer, you also may think about the training that's required to fight. That's how I started to look at my life, as one big training session. The trials and tribulations that I had endured were preparing me for something greater. They were preparing me to *live*.

Giving up is so easy, but I knew that my life was worth fighting for. I knew that I needed to have the courage to confront others who couldn't understand my decisions. I was no longer willing to live with the mistakes that came from listening to other people's opinions. But I could live with the mistakes that were my own doing. The great thing about mistakes is that there really aren't any. Mistakes are just life's lessons in disguise. I have learned to appreciate the lessons that life has taught me. In fact, I've learned more from life than from my college education. Are you willing to take all that you have learned from life and allow it to create a new you? Nothing happens by chance, but what you do with it is up to you. Fighting for your life could mean different things for different people. To me its living free, living in liberty, and living totally removed from the bondage from my past. I'm still learning to embrace my life's teachings and still learning to forgive myself for my old destructive behavior. I would get bothered whenever someone mentioned my past, and I eventually realized that I still needed to forgive myself. There are very few people who know how to truly get underneath my skin, but as I continue to heal from my past, the fewer people can use my past against me. Allow your past to be the problem of others; you should continue to be free. Once you lay your burdens down, DO NOT pick them back up.

Picking up your baggage could be a fight for you. Whenever you decide to pick up your baggage, you are giving yourself permission to relive the pain, heartache, and drama all over again. Have the courage to leave it in the past. The past will kill you, the now will kill you, and the thoughts that you have will kill you if you're not strong enough to confront yourself with the REAL YOU. Don't be in denial. Look at yourself in the mirror and confront everything that tries to destroy you. Take the power of being silent away. My insecurities tried to control me, but I have called them all out, and now they cannot impact me.

Marita, you were a teenage mom.

Marita, you were married three times (divorced and widowed).

Marita, your new husband hates you because he's your third husband.

Marita, everyone hates you because you remarried.

Marita, your children have different last names.

Marita, you used to get high.

Marita, aren't you mad that your brother was murdered?

Marita, your older siblings have disowned you.

Marita, you'll never get over losing your father.

Marita, you're not good enough to write books.

Marita, you come from a broken family.

Hallelujah. The enemy has tried to throw any and all these things in my mind, and I had to ask God to take control over my thoughts and show me who I really was in Him. Once I knew who I was in Christ, I knew that I had the power to fight for my life. It's easy to say that God is good when your life is good. But have you ever been in a place in your life where nothing seems to be good, and you find yourself having nothing but your faith? I mean when you find yourself living in a dark place, and you cannot see the light at the end of the tunnel, and you start to wonder "Where is my God now?" Have you ever been there?

The biggest lie that we believe is that we have no power. My husband, Pastor Demoine Kinney, tells us all the time that people believe in God but struggle with believing in the power of God. Once you have Christ living inside of you as a believer and follower of the gospel, you then begin to realize that you don't operate on your own strength. Instead you allow the Holy Spirit to guide you through your day-to-day life. Therefore, whenever life seems to be overwhelming, take a moment to analyze whether you're walking in the spirit or if your flesh is trying to control you. The flesh always wants to be 'King" in your life and lead you. Whenever you try to do God's job, you'll always end up frustrated. It's not your job to figure out the details of your life. Worrying about this, or about how you're going to pay that. It's your job to trust God in everything and trust Him alone! The fight is not over. In fact it has just begun. You have spent too much time living in the state of defeat. I'm here to tell you that the devil is a liar, and you are not defeated.

No, in all these things we are more than conquerors through him who loved us.
Romans 8:37

Chapter Seventeen: Standards for Your Children

We have a responsibility when we raise our children to help them in every area that we can, and give them everything that we have to give them. I say that because a lot of times we get very hard on ourselves as mothers, but I want you to realize that you can't give your children something you don't have. For years, I really beat myself up because I wanted to give my children things that I didn't have.

I'm not talking about material things. I gave my children every ounce of me, but I realized there were some things that I did not know yet or hadn't developed yet as a mother to give them. When I started taking responsibility for my motherhood, it actually helped me to become a better mother, instead of making an excuse as to why I couldn't do this or I couldn't do that. I remember telling my children, "You guys, I really want you to forgive me for different parts in my life, because I did not know then what I know now."

I would sit down and explain my situation to them, because I was a teenage mom and I had my oldest child when I was 18 years old, but I had my youngest child when I was 30. That's a huge age difference. Marita as an

18-year-old mother was different from the Marita who had a child at 30 years old. I did not know at 18 what I knew at 30. I remember talking to my older children and saying, "I didn't know these things that I know now when I had you, but I did the best that I could with what I had at that moment."

I took responsibility for my children and where I was. I wasn't in denial anymore, and I realized that some of the areas where I felt that I had missed the mark had a lot to do with my maturity and where I was at the time. Especially for those in a blended family situation, women who have children need to have different arrangements with the father emotionally and things like that. It's very difficult when you're immature.

You may not handle things as you would if you were an older, seasoned, grown woman, because when you're a grown woman, you're a different caliber of woman. You carry yourself differently. You mother differently. You nurture differently, and I want my children to know that who I am in my 30s isn't the same person that I was in my early teens and 20s. I explained that to them, because I needed them to know and I didn't want my children to grow up and say "Well, mom did this for you, but she didn't do that for us."

There's a reason I had my children at different stages of my life. When you begin to take responsibility for your children, you are taking responsibility for everything, the good, the bad, the learning experiences, the failures, everything. Financially, you have to set a standard, and the standard that I had set for my children was that I was going to give them what I had and what I didn't have, I prayed that they would be able to pass on to their children.

What I mean by that is that I remember a time with my oldest son where I had said, "Everything that I wasn't able to do for you, I pray that when you have children you're able to do those things for your children that I wasn't able to do for you." It definitely made sense because I believe each generation is supposed to get better than the generation before. It made sense that I pass everything on to my children so they will have it, they would get it.

They will have those chapters and that foundation to build upon. When you take responsibility for them and set that standard of motherhood, you have to take responsibility for what your children have seen you do. I'm not talking about you telling them what to do, but you have to take responsibility for what your children see you do and the life you live in front of them and set those standards. It doesn't matter if it's good or bad.

My children know that I'm a pastor's wife, obviously, but they also know that I'm not a person who lives a double life. I'm a woman who truly serves God daily, and it's in my lifestyle. It's not just on Sundays, and because I choose to be real every day of my life, my children see their mother in her most authentic state. They see things that my friends don't see.

They see things sometimes that even that my husband may not see. My standard was that I would love my children, that I would be there for my children, and I would show my children who I am as a person, not only as their mom. A lot of times, our children know us as their parents, but they never have the opportunity to know the essence of who we are.

I'm not talking about having inappropriate conversations with your children as if they were your friends, but I'm saying that my standard for my children is that I want them to know me as a person. This is just like how some parents mentor other children, they know you as that mentor. They know a part of you, although you're not their parent. I said I don't want another child knowing me better than my own children.

It was important that I mentored my children in a sense in addition to being their parent, because I felt as though that's how they could really get to know me. My standard for my children may be different than yours, but when you have a chance, if you're a mother, sit down and write down the standards that you have for your children and what type of mom you really want to be to them.

Chapter Eighteen: Standards for Your Romantic Life

What are the standards that you have for your romantic life? Now, I know this is going to be a really juicy chapter, because you have to have standards when it comes to your romantic life. I will make a disclosure that in this chapter, I'm referring to women who are married.

I know that there are women out there who are reading this book right now who may not be married, but this chapter and this book is specifically for those who are, because I don't want to condone sex outside of marriage, just because I've been there and done that, and it's a whole hot mess. I've had several chapters about overcoming your past to prove it. This chapter is exclusively for the married women when I'm referring to sex. Chew the meat, spit out the bones if you're unmarried.

Anyway, moving forward - taking responsibility and setting standards for your romantic life. Think about what I mentioned earlier in the chapter. You teach people how to treat you, and if you want that king, you have to treat him like a king in order for him to treat you like a queen.

I have a whole other book for single ladies. If you desire to know more about how to get a man, I could tell you how to do that too.

Let me tell you, and I'm not just saying this, but I really believe that there are some really helpful methods in that book. However, taking responsibility for your romantic life as a wife means meeting your husband's needs. Yes, physical needs are a very big part of it. Meeting his needs is a standard. You have to say, "I'm going to selflessly give myself to my husband. When he wants me, I'll be available. I want to physically be attractive to my husband."

I can't tell you exactly what that is, simply because your husband is not my husband. I cannot tell you what my husband wants, because it's none of your business, and that wouldn't be mature or respectful of me. However, I will tell you that setting the standards for your marriage is important, and you have to decide what that looks like for you and your situation. If you want more intimacy with your husband, such as talking and holding hands, you have to do some things on your end too. It's going to take some work.

Listen to him, support him. Believe in his dreams. Don't tear him down. Build him up. There's a book called Love and Respect, which is really good, because most women want love and men want respect. There's a cycle of women who'll say, "Well, I'm not going to respect him, because he doesn't show me love," and a man feels, "Well, I'm not going to show her any love, because she doesn't respect me," and there's this whole cycle.

If you guys have gone through that or are still going through that, you may want to pick up that book, Love and Respect, because it will definitely help you through that, but you have to set some standards for your marriage. Just to give you a standard that I have set for my marriage, I never wanted to not know my husband. I know you guys are like, "What, how do you not know your husband?" Believe it or not, it happens all the time, especially when you raise children. We have a large family, and so a lot of our time is spent raising our children and working in the ministry, as well as businesses that we own.

Life can become really busy, but my husband and I, we set aside dates several times a month so that we can continue to date throughout our marriage, because it's important that we stay connected, and it's important that we continue to see each other as husband and wife, not just mommy and daddy, pastor, first lady, and business partners, but to see each other as husband and wife, two people who love each other tremendously and support each other.

Grown Woman 101

We don't ever want to look at each other and say "all these years have gone by, we have raised all these kids, and now I've got to know who you are." No, we make sure that we continue to date each other regularly, and it's important to us. It's also a standard that we've set for our romantic life, and you have to see what that looks like for you. However, I encourage you, especially if you're married, to look at your romantic life and set a standard and be careful not to compare it to anybody else's, but instead make sure that your standard is custom to you, your situation, and your significant other.

Single Ladies Wanting to be Married

This section is just for you. I have highlighted some topics from my book "Single Ladies" for you to ponder on.

Here are the main things to consider if you truly desire to be a wife.

- Know what you really want.
- Develop a marriage mindset.
- Become Mrs. Right to Attract Mr. Right.
- Work on yourself.
- Believe in his goal, dreams, and visions.
- Check your motivations.
- Don't be clingy or desperate.

Grown Woman 101

- Being sexy is a demeanor, not clothes.
- Remove any bitterness, forgive those who have hurt you.

I cannot go into all the details; however, I highly encourage you to get my book. The readers highly recommend it for all single women.

Advice for Married Women

- Have Sex with your husband as often as possible… it is wisdom. He can only get that affection from you, and to deprive him is opening a door for all the women who wish they were you and wouldn't mind taking your place. Protect your marriage. "Defraud ye not one the other, unless it be with consent for a time only, that ye may give yourselves to fasting and prayer; and come together again, that Satan tempt you not through your lack of self-restraint." 1 Corinthians 7:5
- Be his help meet. Eve was made for Adam, and before she existed, Adam had a purpose.
- Believe in Him.
- Be his wife and don't try to be his Holy Spirit. It's not your job to convict him.
- Pray for your husband daily.
- Choose him daily.
- Recognize and honor the King in him (If you're a Queen, then he must be the King).
- Respect his authority and trust him to lead.

- You owe it to yourself to be a good wife to him... it's for you.
- Provide him with a peaceful home.

I'm going to stop right there. I need to write another book to discuss all of that. Prayerfully those tips will help you in the meantime.

TIME

GROWN WOMEN KNOW HOW TO SPEND THEIR TIME

Chapter Nineteen: Time Management

A grown woman understands that she only has 24 hours in a day, so she must spend her time wisely. Do not waste your time on things that don't matter. We're all given 24 hours in a day. What you do with your time is your business, but you are responsible for how you decide to spend your time. If there are things in your life that you want to do, you are going to make time for them.

You have to make sure that time management is a part of your life, because when you are a grown woman, you understand that your time has to be managed in order for you to even complete all the things that are mentioned in this book. Everything in this book that is part of your life takes time. You are responsible for how you manage it and how you mismanage it. If you're mismanaging your time, sit down, write out a journal, and keep a log of what you do every hour.

Find out where you are mismanaging your time and readjust your schedule so that you are getting the most out of your day, each and every day. I don't care who you are. You are never going to see today again. When you go to sleep and you wake up and it's the next day, the previous day is over and done with. You'll never see it again. It's important that you utilize the time that you have as efficiently as possible so that you can be as productive as possible in every area of your life. A grown woman does not take her time for granted.

OK.

Chapter Twenty: Wasting Time

What do you waste your time on? Oftentimes, it's television and social media. Nowadays, that's most of it, but there are other things that waste people's time. Sometimes it's other people. Is the TV wasting your time? Is social media wasting your time? Is someone in your life wasting your time? Are you wasting your own time? What is it that you're doing that's wasting your time?

I'm telling you right now, we all have been guilty of it, and from time to time I'm guilty of it, but when you're aware of time wasters, it's possible to become very annoyed. When I became more conscientious of my time, I would say "that just wasted my time", and I didn't like that, because I realized that I wasn't going to get that time back. I try to avoid the things that were going to waste my time.

One of the things that I did was cut out TV, and it freed up a lot of time to write. It freed up a lot of time to do things at home, and spend time with my children and my husband. I remember my husband saying to me one time, "You know, we're tired of watching TV and looking at everybody live out their dreams," and I was like "Huh?"

he said, "Think about it. Every time we watch TV, we're watching somebody else live out their dreams." He's said, "I'm ready to live out our dreams. If people want to watch, let them watch, but I'm living out my dreams."

He said, "So Marita, you live out your dream. We've got some dreams that we are trying to live out too. We don't have time to be sitting on the couch watching other people live out their dreams while we are just sitting here wasting time." I promise you, that was one of the truest statements I've ever heard in my life. How many times have we been guilty of just watching other people live out their life? Look, I'm making a declaration. Watch me live, because I don't have time to watch you.

I don't have many regrets, but I do regret all of the times that I allowed other people and things to waste my time. Pay attention, I used the word *allowed* for a reason. I use to have time wasters in my life, and they were draining my energy. Every time they were around me, they used up my useful time. I wasted time giving advice that they were not ready to receive. I wasted my time sharing business information with people who were not serious about investing in themselves. I went places that didn't add any value to my life. I allowed my immaturity to cost me days that I can never get back.

Grown women invest their time wisely, because we understand the value. If the people around you don't respect your time, make them. Set boundaries. I cannot begin to tell you how many women are single right now, simply because they are too available to everyone. Have a life, for heaven's sake. Men still like a chase. Single ladies; don't be so available for these men. I had no idea that I was going to go there, but that sentence was for someone out there reading this book.

Discern who is wasting your time, and move them out of the way. Life is too short to be around people who are hindering you from being productive with your time. Grown women don't have time to be in everyone's business and drama. We're not interested. We conduct business, mind our own business, and start businesses. If you have a messy friend that calls you with gossip, sorry, but she's a time waster. Time is precious, treat it as such.

Single Ladies, Stop Wasting your Time Trying to Find Mr. Right.

When we were kids, we often fantasized about our prince charming. We want nothing but the best. Well, who wouldn't? However, are YOU already the absolute Ms. Right for your Mr. Right? Allow me to answer that question for you. Probably not! In today's world we as women can get so distracted with our day-to-life. We all want the perfect man and yet we're nowhere near to being perfect. It's not fair to want someone with qualities that you have yet to possess for yourself. It's crazy to want a man who drives a nice car and your car stays in the shop and barely runs. You want to man with good credit, but bill collectors are calling your phone day and night. Why would a man with good credit want an irresponsible wife who cannot pay bills on time? Exactly, he wouldn't. You must become who you desire to have. Once you start to become Mrs. Right, the right man will admire the likeness and will automatically have something in common with you. If you enjoy working out, chances are that you'll have a physically fit man interested in you. However, you can't get upset if sloppy men are approaching you, what does that say about you? Singleness does NOT EQUAL Loneliness.

Men are looking for Mrs. Right, just like you're hoping that Mr. Right will find you. A lot of women make the mistake of being TOO OVERLY OCCUPIED. Yep! It's true. You can be your own worst enemy and a distraction for men. We as women have no idea what we have become in the eyes of men. Men want us to be available. What's stopping you from being available and approachable? Is it your phone? Your daily drama? Or is it your friends or work? If you're overly preoccupied men will not approach you. Are you causing yourself to remain single?

Mrs. Right will know how to balance her life and leave room for the man of her dreams. Sometimes woman are guilty of staying busy to prevent themselves from becoming lonely. It sounds good, but if that describes you....I have one question, "Are you still single?" I'm not trying to be harsh. I'm just being honest. Woman who are too busy, also appear to be too busy for a love life in the eyes of men. Do you have time to be courted? Do you have time to be a wife and possibly a mother? Use your time wisely. Remember that you don't have to take up every second of the day trying to stay busy. It's important to know how to be *with yourself* and not *by yourself.*

Mrs. Right will be confident. Most men don't really care how you look. I can't believe I just said that. Well it's true whenever your confident being in your own skin. Men are attracted to confidence more than image. There's nothing worse than being a beautiful woman who lacks self-confidence. Have you ever seen ugly women that are also married? My point exactly. inner beauty is so much prevalent than outer beauty. Who you are at the core is what will make you desirable to men. Don't compare yourself to other women. Embrace who you are and what you have to offer. Last but not least, leave something special for your husband. Don't give men that you are dating your everything. Leave something for your King. If you don't, what's going to make him any different from the rest of the men.

Chapter Twenty One: Productive Time

Everybody wants productive day. Everybody wants that. However, a busy day is not necessarily a productive day, so you have to make sure that what you're doing with your time is productive. How do you determine if it's productive? Ask yourself, does what I'm doing matter? If you're just busy for the sake of being busy, and you're just wasting time without any benefit to your life, it's not productive. You're just busy.

That's a time waster as well, but when you choose to have a productive life, there may be only three things that you do in a day, but they are important, they add value, and they mean something. One of the ways to ensure that you have a productive day is to write down a list of things to do for the next day the night before. The problem with doing it in the morning time is that your day has already started, and you have to take the time to make a to-do list, so you've already wasted time just to make your to-do list when you could have already started working on your list.

What I do oftentimes, what I suggest you do, and what many millionaires also do is to write down our to-do list in the evening or make a mental note, so that when you wake up in the morning, you already know what it is you have to do. You don't have to sit there and try to figure it out and then write it down, because that's just a waste of time.

You wake up with your game plan already in mind and you can start on it immediately. You can start your to-do list the night before, wake up, start working on it, making sure that what you're doing is important to you and that you're not just staying busy. Time is important and you'll never get it back, so make sure that you're using it wisely.

Everything that you do should have a meaning behind it. If it doesn't have a meaning, it probably isn't helping you to be productive. Grown women understand the difference between being busy and being productive. If you're busy for no reason, doing things for absolutely for no purpose, you may have a major issue. If this is you, ask yourself, "Why can't I be alone with myself? What are the things that I'm trying to avoid? Why am I working so hard?" Usually, something is going on inside you. Are you insecure? Are you afraid of something? Are you trying to prove a point to someone? I don't know the answers to those questions, but you do. Whatever you do with your time, make sure that you always challenge the motive behind it.

Chapter Twenty Two: The Best Way to Chill Out!

Everyday life can become overwhelming, and the need to relax becomes apparent. The problem remains in the way you chose to take a break from your hectic schedule. Whenever people are stressed out, attitudes and irritability follow. No one enjoys being around a cranky person. If you find yourself becoming angry with any and every one, chances are, you may need to take a chill pill. Taking a vacation seems to be the easiest solution. However, planning for a vacation can end up contributing to even more stress. So what is the best way to chill? That's a great question and I'm about to help you with that in this article. First ask yourself these questions.

- Would you enjoy being around *you*?
- Do you over commit?
- Are you easily frustrated?
- How often do you get alone time?
- Are you mean to those around you?
- Do you find yourself complaining often?
- Is it hard for you to relax?

Grown Woman 101

- Do you cope with life instead of living it to the fullest?

If you're easily irritated, you may not be a jerk after all. Stress can cause people to become unkind. The key is for you to find balance in your life. Most of us work, but forget to chill out. By doing so, we tend to take out our frustrations on the people closest to us. The solution is you. Your body is telling you to relax and regroup.

The best way to chill isn't in planning long vacations, or traveling miles away, or spending a large amount of money. I know what you may be thinking - how is that so? Well, don't get me wrong, I love vacations, traveling, and shopping, but all of those activities can leave you feeling exhausted. It doesn't take much planning to relax. Actually, it's encouraged to relax regularly. instead of taking an annual vacation. Here are some simple ways to relax in your everyday life.

- Take a walk
- Read a book
- Listen to nature
- Get some sunlight
- Journal your thoughts
- Turn off your cell phone

Marita Kinney
Page 149

- Take a break from social media
- Take a nap
- Laugh
- Get a massage
- Prioritize your daily tasks
- Create an oasis at home

There are many ways to relax. However, none of them matter if you don't make the time to do it. Prioritizing your day is essential and it starts with you. It's common to put yourself last, but neglecting yourself should never been an option.

After relaxing, you will have the energy to become more productive and creative. Doing too much at once will limit your ability, preventing you from reaching your greatest potential. We all get 24 hours in a day, but how you use it is up to you. Life is busy and can leave you feeling burnt out. Who said that you have to wait for a vacation? You can create your own oasis at home. Everyone should have that one special spot where you can breathe and let go of the issues of the day. Your happiness is in the way you value your life. Treat yourself well and give yourself a break.

Time to Play - having fun adds balance to your life.

Time to Prioritize - As life changes, so will your priorities.

Chapter Twenty Three: Becoming a Grown Woman

I'm not sure how old you are as you read this book, but what I will tell you is that becoming a grown woman is about looking at life and realizing that it's nothing but lessons. Just like I've shared different lessons with you in this book, your life is a book of chapters that is full of lessons, and how you utilize that entire book will give your life so much meaning, so much power, so much to offer the world, other people, and yourself.

A grown woman takes responsibility for her life, for her love, for her children, for her time, for her creativity. Every failure and every success is used to her benefit. Grown women don't have pity parties. We dust ourselves off. We learn the chapters that we meant to learn from, and we move on. Grown women love intentionally as if we've never been hurt. Although we may have been hurt a thousand times, we intentionally love again.

We intentionally better ourselves every day. A truly extraordinary grown woman realizes that she's never arrived, yet she's evolving every day, willing to learn, willing to grow, willing to press through her tears, willing to press through her pain, willing to make peace with her past, willing to embrace who she is, acknowledge where she's been, and prepare for where she is going.

Someone once asked me, "Marita, who do you admire the most?" I said humbly, "I admire myself. I admire the person that I'm becoming and I can't wait to meet her, because I know her entire story." I said the reason why I can't admire anyone else is because I don't know their whole story. People only tell you what they want you to know, but I can't hide from myself. I know every detail of my life, the whole truth and nothing but the truth and I admire that person. I admire her strength. I admire her struggle. I admire everything that she's overcome, and that's why I admire the woman that I'm becoming.

I ask that you look over your life today and really take the lessons in this book as a template. For every chapter that was mentioned in this book, customize it, make it personal, and go through your own life and think about what you could take responsibility for and the standards of life that you could set for yourself to become not only the extraordinary woman that you're becoming, but the extraordinary woman that you are starting to acknowledge. You already know that you're great. Now it's time to show the world exactly who you are. I love you. God bless. Be encouraged and be extraordinarily you.

Chapter Twenty Four: Courage

Do You Have the Courage to Be You?

We live in an era where you can be anything that you desire to be, but it takes courage to be yourself. A lot of people struggle with identity and are defined by their accomplishments, family orientation, social status, or their associations. If you were to remove all of those dynamics from your life, who would you be? Are you comfortable being you, even if others don't approve of your choices and decisions? Living based on the approval of other people is a sure way to lose sight of who you are. You will always get the short end of the stick if you choose to live that way.

Living with regrets will make your life feel unfulfilled and meaningless. Have you ever said to yourself, "I wish, I would have, I should have, done XYZ?" Of course, we all have, and unknown possibilities are likely to become our road blocks.

- Fear of failure

- Fear of being different

- Fear of success

- Fear of rejection

- Fear of being judged

And the list goes on, adding to the factors which cause you to limit your potential for being the very best you. However, what if you replaced the word "fear" with "courage to,"
Who would you be?

- Courage to fail (at least you have tried)

- Courage to be different (at least you're authentic)

- Courage to be successful (at least you have found your passion)

- Courage to be rejected (at least you're accepted within)

- Courage to be judged (at least they're paying attention)

It takes strength and courage to move forward in life and to face the possibility of not meeting the expectations of other people. I have learned that even my failures turned out to be a success. Life is the best teacher, and learning from "your own" experience and mistakes is hands-on-training. Are you willing to take your life's chapters and apply them to the real you? What has life taught you, and do you have the courage to explore what to do with the experience you have been given? Your experience is connected to your passion, your passion is connected to your purpose, and your purpose is the key to who you are and what you should be doing. Do not compare your life to other people. You already have everything in you that you need for who you should be "at this" moment in your life. As time continues to pass, you'll experience more and should apply more of life's chapters. You'll continue to grow with your experiences, and will need the courage and knowledge to blossom into your unique self. No one can be you better than yourself. Make the decision today to accept and love who you are, and who you are not.

Chapter Twenty Five: Your Appearance

What does your appearance say about you? Does it truly represent who you are? I have worked from home since 2007. It takes a lot of focus and discipline. I remember one of my friends stopping by because she was in the area. We didn't live in the same city, so her visit was pleasantly welcomed. Not everyone has the privilege of just popping up at my house, but there are a few people who are an exception to the rule. I can still remember the look on her face as I opened the door. I was elegantly dressed in business casual attire, my make-up was flawless, and my hair just in place.

My appearance caught her off guard. After we hugged and greeted each other, she couldn't help but mention her thoughts regarding my appearance. "Marita, I know that you're sharp and always on point. However, I had no idea that you dress like this as you work from home. I was expecting you to open the door in some sweat pants." We both began to laugh. Then, I realized that she didn't know me at the core. Most women dress nicely for each other. Some women want compliments, some want to make a statement, and some women want to compete with others. It didn't dawn on my friend that I dress to impress myself and no one else.

Grown Woman 101

It's important that you understand why you do the things that you do. I'm the same person, with or without an audience. I carry myself with the same demeanor every day of the week. Please don't judge yourself based on my example. When I work from home, I create a realistic work environment, because it improves my overall performance. If I happen to leave my house throughout the day, people take me seriously when I introduce myself. So, I ask you again, who is representing you? When my niece came to live with us, she asked me why I dressed up every time I left the house. I replied, "Because I never know who I'm going to meet or do business with. You only get one time to make a first impression." I then went on to say, "If I wore any old thing in my closet and looked a hot mess, would anyone believe that I'm a best-selling author, a publisher, and own a Café?" Her face said it all. She finally understood that in order for people to take you seriously, you must take yourself seriously first.

Changing habits is difficult, but I was determined to become the best version of myself. I began to get rid of clothes that I could simply throw on to run out to the store. If the clothes were there, I was often tempted to not represent myself well. I used to get so angry at myself, because I would meet someone or run into someone I knew on my worst-dressed days. I would get so embarrassed, until finally my entire wardrobe represented where I was going. Sometimes, we get so caught up in where we are that we lose focus of where we desire to go in life.

- You have to dress for the position you want.
- Act as if you belong where you desire to go.
- Begin to set expectations for your image.
- Don't try to be like anyone but yourself.

I grew up in the hood, but it didn't determine how I saw myself. I saw myself as a business woman, not one of the girls that walked around wearing bedroom shoes and scarves on my head. You have to make a choice. You are the one that gets to decide how you dress, not your environment. Not all young men in the hood sag their pants. Some of those young men have made a choice to wear their clothes with prestige, no matter how much the clothes cost. It not about cost, it's about mindset.

You don't have to go on a shopping spree to change your overall appearance. All you have to do is wear your clothes differently. Begin to experiment with what you already have. But first, you have to decide what look you desire to have to best represents your TRUE SELF. As you grow and change, your image will as well. You should not have the same style that you had twenty years ago. Figure out who you are today as a woman, and represent her.

Change

Your body is going to change, get over it. When I was younger, I couldn't wait to gain a few extra pounds. I wanted to have curves in all the right places. For some reason, I didn't take into consideration that after having five natural children, my body would drastically change. I used to actually brag about not having any stretch marks. Well, I spoke too soon. When baby number four came, she left my mommy war marks, also known as "stretch marks." I wasn't insecure after obtaining them; I just had to get used to my new body. I was a mom who had given birth multiple times, which resulted in my body changing. I thought to myself, "Who cares? I'm a woman."

Dealing with Heartbreak

As a woman, I know that heartbreak is one of the toughest issues that we'll ever face. There are numerous types of heartbreak. Some involve our love life, relationships with parents, friendships, disappointment in children, and for many more, there is heartbreak due to death.

No one can escape death. At some point in time, we will all die or lose someone. It's by far the hardest reality of life for most of us.

I have experience all kinds of heartbreak, but whenever someone died that was close to me, I had to rearrange my life. If you have lost a loved one, then you understand the pain that I'm referring to. The pain that comes and goes, but stings at the very thought of living life without that person. Fear sets in, and the unknown appears.

There is no pain like having a broken heart. Have you ever heard of someone going to the doctor because their heart was broken? There are counselors and therapists, yes, but you still have to do the work in order to move forward. Heartbreak can destroy a woman's soul. I know. One day, I was at my breaking point. My heart had been broken time and time again, until I realized that I couldn't control heartbreak. However, I could control how I reacted to it. My twenties were a difficult time for me. My brother was killed in a robbery and my father died from diabetes, and at the same time I left my first husband, remarried, and ended up being a widow at the age of 26. My second husband died from cancer suddenly, and I was emotionally drained. My oldest son kept begging me to let him live with his father, but the divorce left a bitter taste in my mouth for his dad. I couldn't stand his father; in the midst of my stubbornness, I must have forgotten that his relationship with his father wasn't contingent on my ill feelings. Hurt people hurt others. When you're hurting, you don't see the pain that you're afflicting others. You cannot allow your pain be passed down. A grown woman must decide to separate her feelings in order to make mature decisions. I began to ask God to remove all of my heartbreak and life's disappointments, because they were robbing me of my future.

Realizing that you have a choice gives you power. I was choosing to deal with heart break in the wrong manner. Before I gained more wisdom, I handled it with an attitude, with marijuana, with isolation, with carelessness, and with no cautiousness. Once I became aware of my actions, I soon discovered that I was pouring salt in my own wounds. Life hurt me and left me broken, and I had no idea that I was hurting myself too. I wasn't any better to myself. Learning to love myself was essential to my success as a woman. I learned to find peace in the middle of my storms, and you can too.

Children:

There is no greater heartbreak than a mother's heart breaking over her children. I remember growing up and watching my mother grieve from the terrible decisions that my brother made. I didn't understand it at first. I couldn't understand why his choices affected her so much. Then my brother was killed. My mother always told me, "Marita there is no pain, like the pain of a mother who has lost a child." I felt bad for her. Mothers can move on, but they remain scared forever. This applies to women who have also experienced miscarriages, and other infant deaths such as abortions. I find myself reminding the woman who don't have any *living* children, that no matter what, they're still a mother. There now a mother who has lost their child, but they're still a mother.

Children have a way of hurting you to the core. Sometimes that hurt forms from the child's disrespect, unloving behavior, disobedience, stealing, belittling, being unappreciative, and the list goes on. Spoiled kids can become the meanest kids. As a mother, it's your job to be a parent first. Your kid may not like you, but your job is to guide, teach, and love them. Not to please them or become their closest pal. I know all too well. Being a parent takes a lot of courage. You have to stand up to your children and demand respect from them. The overall goal is to raise respectable, independent, adults. Children need a parent. They are not supposed to raise themselves. Don't allow your child to bully you. Remind them who the parent is and who is the child. They'll thank you later. Whatever the outcome may be, they'll have to also take 100% for all of the information and guidance that you have given. Each generation should get better. Teach your child to build upon your mistakes and use them as stepping stones to reach a higher level in life.

Grown Woman 101

Grown Woman Advice:

1. Don't allow someone to change your attitude because of their ignorance. Be a lady at all times. However, if you need to check someone, do it by improving your success and personal growth. Grown women don't waste time on messy women.

2. Grown women don't gossip. We're not involved in other people's business, because we're busy taking care of business... our home, finances, relationships, career, goals, education, etc.

3. Grown women don't make mistakes, because it's always an opportunity to learn and grow. It's all about perception.

4. Remind yourself that you have no competition. There is only one you, and no one can be you better than yourself. Besides, it's the best gift that you can give yourself.

5. Decide to grow every day.

6. A grown woman is also a student and a teacher. Learn and teach along the way.

7. You don't have to be loud to be heard.

8. When you speak, have something to say.

9. Love as if you were never hurt.

10. All others to love you.

11. Seek God and everything else will fall into place.

12. Arrive every day, and show up to conquer your fears.

13. Be a lady, it never goes out of style.

14. The Best thing you can wear is a smile.

Grown Women are just Little Girls Who

Have Decided to Grow Up and Take

Responsibility for their Life.

-Marita Kinney

How to Become a Godly Woman

1. SEEK GOD FIRST: Reject the lie that anything or anyone else can satisfy you.

"But seek first His kingdom and His righteousness, and all these things will be added to you. So do not worry about tomorrow; for tomorrow will care for itself. Each day has enough trouble of its own." – Matthew 6:33-34

Other Scripture:

1 Chronicles 16:8-12, Psalm 9:10, Psalm 27:1-5, Psalm 34:10-14, Psalm 40:16, Jeremiah 29:11-13, Zephaniah 2:3, Matthew 6:25-34

2. SPEAK FAITHFULLY: Love others with godly wisdom, boldness, and kindness as a faithful completer of others.

Then the LORD God said, "It is not good for the man to be alone; I will make him a helper suitable for him." – Genesis 2:18

Better is open rebuke than love that is concealed. Faithful are the wounds of a friend, but deceitful are the kisses of an enemy. – Proverbs 27:5-6

Open your mouth for the mute, for the rights of all the unfortunate. Open your mouth, judge righteously, and defend the rights of the afflicted and needy. – Proverbs 31:8-9

She opens her mouth in wisdom, and the teaching of kindness is on her tongue. – Proverbs 31:26

Psalms 19:14, Proverbs 12:18, Proverbs 13:3, Proverbs 16:13, Proverbs 20:15, Proverbs 24:26

3. SHOW TRUE BEAUTY: Bodies deteriorate, people develop. Invest in that which lasts.

Charm is deceitful and beauty is vain, but a woman who fears the LORD, she shall be praised. – Proverbs 31:30

Likewise, I want women to adorn themselves with proper clothing, modestly and discreetly, not with braided hair and gold or pearls or costly garments, but rather by means of good works, as is proper for women making a claim to godliness. – 1 Timothy 2:9-10

1 Samuel 16:7, Proverbs 11:22,1 Peter 3:3-5

4. STAY HUMBLE: Be constantly aware of pride and selfishness. Don't think less of yourself, but think of yourself less.

"Has not my hand made all these things, and so they came into being?" declares the LORD. "These arc the ones I look on with favor: those who are humble and contrite in spirit, and who tremble at my word." – Isaiah 66:2

Do nothing from selfishness or empty conceit, but with humility of mind regard one another as more important than yourselves; do not merely look out for your own personal interests, but also for the interests of others. Have this attitude in yourselves which was also in Christ Jesus. – Philippians 2:3-5

Psalm 141:5, Proverbs 3:5-6, Proverbs 12:1, Micah 6:8, John 15:5, 1 Peter 3:8-9,1 Peter 5:5-7

5. SERVE THE LORD: Set your mind on eternal things, serve the eternal King, live to please only Him.

"He who loves his life loses it, and he who hates his life in this world will keep it to life eternal. If anyone serves Me, he must follow Me; and where I am, there My servant will be also; if anyone serves Me, the Father will honor him." – John 12:25-26

Grown Woman 101

For am I now seeking the favor of men, or of God? Or am I striving to please men? If I were still trying to please men, I would not be a bond-servant of Christ. – Galatians 1:10

Whatever you do, do your work heartily, as for the Lord rather than for men. – Colossians 3:23

Psalm 16:11, Psalm 84:10-12, Mark 10:42-45,2

Corinthians 5:10, Philippians 1:21, Hebrews 6:10,1 Peter 2:21-23

What Your Mother May Not Have Taught

You

Sometimes it's easiest to blame what we don't know on our mothers. We complain about our short comings, instead of finding the proper resources to improve them. I don't claim to be an expert in this field, but I'm a mother and want to share what I have learned. I often talk with my closest friends, and we have realized that our mothers couldn't give us what they didn't have. Therefore, whatever you learn, pay it forward.

Dress Code

SMART CASUAL

Wear a pencil skirt or dress pants, paired with a silk or button-down top and high heels.

When to wear it: office parties, happy hours, business luncheons.

DRESSY CASUAL

Avoid wearing denim, tennis shoes, and cotton tees. Instead, opt for silk pants, dress pants, or a skirt. Pair with a patent leather flat, or one with nice embellishments such as a bow, buckle, or a print.

When to wear it: church, dinner, or an invite received via phone or e-mail.

COUNTRY CLUB CASUAL

Choose an open-necked or polo shirt. You can also opt for dresses and skirts with minimal accessories.

When to wear it: cruise lines, the country club, friend's home for dinner, nice restaurant.

BUSINESS CASUAL

Put on a skirt, khakis, or dress pants paired with long sleeve or three-quarter sleeve tops. A casual dress and flats are options as well.

When to wear it: company party, daily work attire, business lunch meetings.

COCKTAIL ATTIRE

Wear a shorter dress with some frill. The classic little black dress makes for great cocktail attire, and is the easiest to show your personality by accessorizing to suit your mood.

When to wear it: adult birthday parties, evening social events.

LOUNGE

Wear a dress that would be appropriate for brunch or afternoon tea. It should fall to, or slightly above, the knee, and not be too sparkly or low-cut. Incorporate a jacket or shawl to cover the arms.

When to wear it: daytime engagement parties, business breakfasts, afternoon tea.

WHITE TIE

A floor-length ball gown is a must. Accessorize with opera length gloves, glamorous jewels, and up-do hairstyles.

When to wear it: charity fundraisers, government ceremonies, weddings, the opera.

BLACK TIE

Gussy up in a floor-length ball gown. A very dressy cocktail dress may be acceptable depending on the venue of the event.

When to wear it: charity fundraisers, political dinner parties, weddings.

CREATIVE BLACK TIE

Women: Dress up in a long gown, cocktail dress, or snazzy separates. Accessorize with the latest trends, such as feathers, sequins, sheer fabrics, and capes. Show off your personality with every detail.

When to wear it: galas, silent auctions, weddings, and formal dinners that have a fun atmosphere.

WARM WEATHER BLACK TIE

Wear a long gown with white gloves and minimal jewelry.

When to wear it: formal events that are held outdoors, such as a cruise line or country club dinners, weddings, and galas.

BLACK TIE OPTIONAL

Look glamorous in a long gown, cocktail dress, or luxurious separates. Accessorize with items such as long gloves, clutches, and jewelry to top off the whole look.

When to wear it: elegant events such as galas, silent auctions, weddings, formal dinners.

Jewelry

Choosing Jewelry for Necklines

Sweetheart: Curved

Turtlenck: Long Chain/Pendant

Crew: Bib or Collar

Scoop: Shorter with volume

Strapless: Choker

Square: Angular Pendants

Cowl: Earrings

Off Shoulder: Asymmetric

Halter: Stem Pendant

V Neck: V Shape

Collar: Short Pendant/Choker

Boatneck: Long Chain/Beads

How to Set a Table

INFORMAL

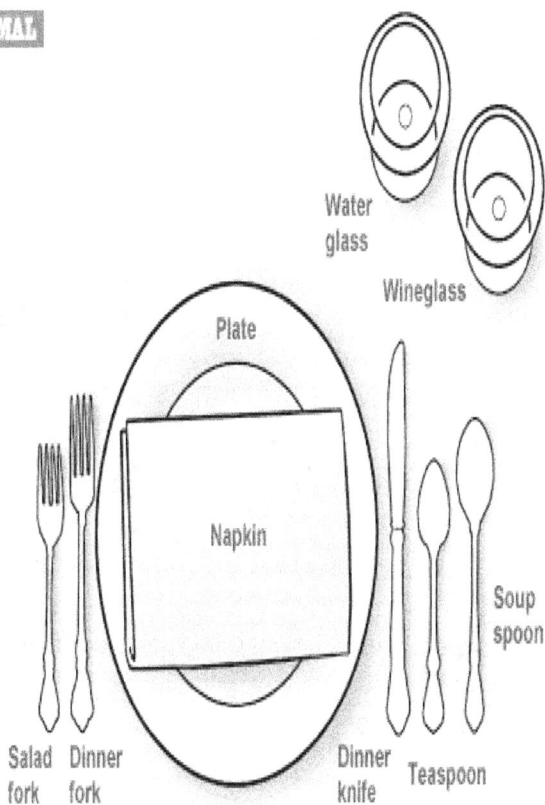

Water glass

Wineglass

Plate

Napkin

Soup spoon

Salad fork   Dinner fork

Dinner knife   Teaspoon

Utensils are placed one inch from the edge of the table

Grown Woman 101

Undergarments

- Make sure that your panties and bras match.
- Wear a body shaper, not because you're fat...but because it looks tacky to have your booty wiggling when you walk.
- Don't always buy panties in a bag. Sometimes treat yourself to some from Victoria's Secret, or at least some that hang on a hanger.
- Thongs are fine to wear, but make sure that they're not exposed.
- Wear bras that fit. Don't have your breasts falling out.
- No panty lines. We should not be able to tell what kind of panties you are wearing.
- Wear lingerie or sexy night clothes often (it's so ladylike).
- Bodysuits are cute, provide body control, and are super sexy. Don't worry - married ladies, they have crotchless ones too.

Perfume

- Find your scent, a fragrance that smells nice on you.
- Put perfume on your wrist, behind your knees, behind your earlobes, and on your neck. This will leave your scent lingering, but not overwhelming.
- Difference between Toilette and Perfume:
The **differences** are simply a matter of the amount or concentration of oils in the fragrance. The highest concentration is in pure **perfume** (or **parfum**). Next would be Eau de **Parfum**, then Eau de **Toilette**, and finally Eau de Cologne.

Make-up

How to apply make-up for your face shape

House Cleaning

•Cleaning Schedule•

Weekly

Monday
Bedrooms

Tuesday
Kitchen: counters, fridge
Microwave, floors

Wednesday
Laundry: Wash, Fold, Put Away

Tursday
Bathrooms: counters, floors, tubs,
mirrors, toilets

Friday
Living/Office: dust, vaccum

Saturday
Swing

Sunday
Laundry: wash, fold, put away
Launder sheets & towels
Vaccum + Furniture

Monthly

Dust ceiling fans
Wipe out trash cans
Wipe down switches
Sanitize door knobs
Dog's medicine
Change air filter
Wipe down vents
Vacuum under cushions
Vacuum ceiling corners
Clean cycle dishwasher
Clean cycle washing
machine

Quarterly

Vacuum mattresses
Launder comforters
Launder shower curtains
Launder drapes
Clean oven
Descale Keurig

Signed! Today more and more people download books and don't have the opportunity to have them signed.
Thank you for your support, and you do have a signed copy!!!

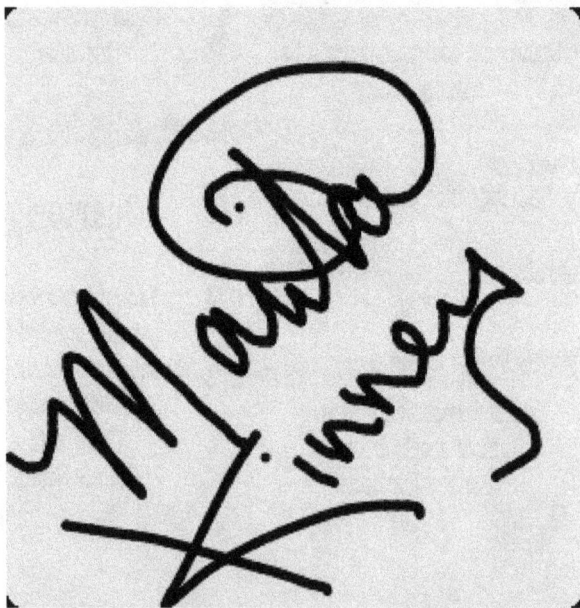

About the Author:

Marita L Kinney is an Best-Selling Author and a woman of many talents. A published Author, Life Coach and Motivational Speaker, and of course a entrepreneur, Marita has inspired thousands of people to overcome adversity with triumph through faith and perseverance. While facing several life changing challenges herself, Marita had enough faith to conquer tribulations, coming out victorious. She is best known for her Christian Fiction novellas and heart felt inspirational books. Loving God with her whole heart, she has vowed to live a life of transparency winning souls to Christ with the realness of her journey and the relatability of her testimony. In March of 2009 Marita published her debut book "The Unspoken Walk". Capturing the true essence of what it means to turn "lemons into lemonade", she has taken the harsh lessons of life and developed a plan for successfully living.

More Books by Marita:

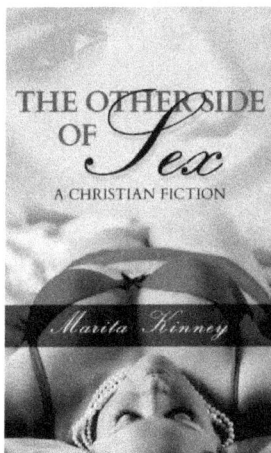

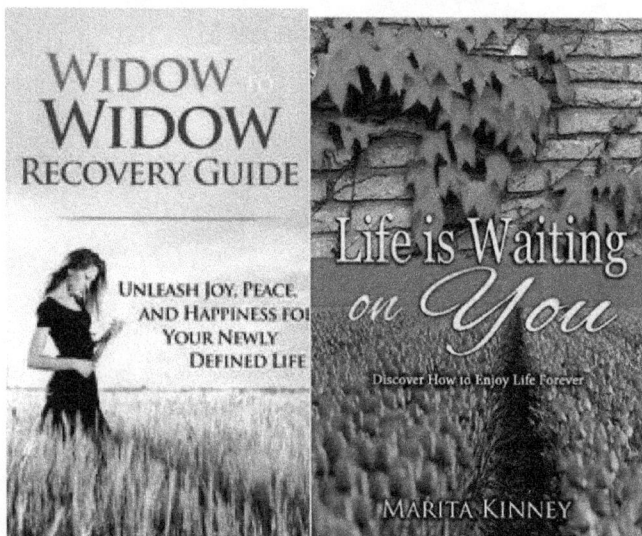

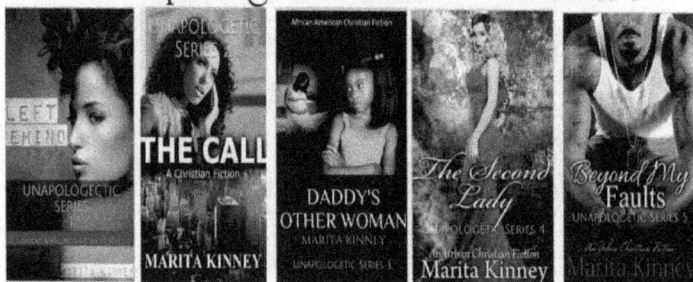

Booking Request

www.maritakinney.com

info@maritakinney

www.ingramcontent.com/pod-product-compliance
Lightning Source LLC
Chambersburg PA
CBHW031547040426
42452CB00006B/222